PATRON
SAINT
of
MISFITS

PATRON
SAINT
of
MISFITS

The Truth WILL Set You Free...
But First It Makes You Crazy

T. AVILA

Xulon Press
2301 Lucien Way #415
Maitland, FL 32751
407.339.4217
www.xulonpress.com

Printed in the United States of America.

ISBN-13: 9781545644096

The brokenhearted, orphaned, abused, wounded, desperate, crippled,
depressed, crazy, drunk, maimed, hopeless, and brave.

The homeless, lonely, forgotten, afflicted, sorrowful, grieving, suffering,
no matter what we drink, take, eat, buy, kiss, steal, see or hear.

For wounded heart people everywhere.
And for those who love us anyway. Who want to understand and help us.

There will be stars in your crown.

What *is* love? Do we tap dance to get it? Or rebel against it?
Or look in godawful places for what we *think* is love?

We *want* to be joyful and positive, aglow in wonder and awe.
Some of us are even pretty good at pretending.

But we grieve our childhood wounds, hide our secret shame,
limp through days crushed by sorrow.

And are heartsick that we flapped our wings, but never flew.
It seems to us that once people *could* fly, that *we* even planned to.
And we have a secret well of sadness that we can't.

This book is for us.

"THE LORD IS NEAR
THE BROKEN HEARTED
AND SAVES THOSE
WHO ARE CRUSHED
IN SPIRIT."

Psalms 34:18 (NIV)

With Gratitude Forever To
Ran Stovall
"Christian Family Counseling"
Thank you for saving my life
By teaching me about the One who owns it
And speaking for Him when I could not recognize His voice

TABLE OF CONTENTS

ALL SHALL BE WELL

Introduction

If we are misfits, we know it by now.
People hurt us. Or left us.
Dreams withered on the vine.
The crooked path nothing like the early dream.
These are our stories.
And God's.
How we came to be wounded.
And what God did about it.

There's a twelve-step program for almost everything, seems like. But not for Misfits. Not one for, "I'm so lost, why did that happen, why was I ever born, what do I do now?"

I'm eleven-and-a-half steps along on that journey, and want to share what I've learned. There are a lot of us out here, and I've had more help than most. There's something about having your own life saved that makes you want to share the life preserver.

This book is not a MEmoir. It is a WEmoir. My own story, and the stories of other wounded people I have known. Part "memoir," part "self-help." We all have wounds, just find different "Band-Aids" to put on them – drugs, food, sex, gambling...whatever we find that eases the pain. Then comes the *worse* pain. And we are lost.

1

Trauma is a fact of life. One out of four of us grew up with alcoholic parents, one in five have been molested, and a third of all couples have suffered from physical violence in their relationship. We live a long way downstream from the cross and the world isn't gettin' any prettier. Science is proving that the brain of a trauma survivor does not look normal on an MRI. Not quite like the others. The body remembers even when our mind hides it all away.

This book began with a deep longing, begging the Lord: "Please do not let it all be for nothing." My own struggle, and all the wounded souls I've known and loved. God's answers saved our lives. Over the years He taught me who I really was in Him, not who the world said I was by my wounds. He brought the things I *could* do and never mentioned the ones I *couldn't*. Taught me to *give* what I never *got* and be healed.

Telling our stories to God is where we start. Secrets and shame need His light, whether it is from our sins or the sins done to us. Keepin' it real, tellin' it like it really is. Not like we *pretend* it is. Telling it straight-up to *God*. And learning how to let God wrap His story around it.

There's a lot we can study about God – theology, history, churches, doctrines.

This is not that kind of book.

Nor is this another sweet little inspirational book about faith and blessings – people who get what they pray for and everyone is happy. No. It is about the unspeakable traumas some of us suffer in this fallen world. And how to turn our wounds into wings.

It is grounded in scripture for sure, but in a way that His Spirit wants you to *know* Him. Know Him in a way that *connects* us to Him, whether we are dyslexics, PhDs, suffer from Down syndrome, have a brain tumor, are math nerds or librarians.

We need to *know* God...not know *about* Him. Have a *relationship* with Him that is intimate and tailored just to us. In a way that enables those of us born into *broken* love to finally experience *perfect* love.

What is *your* story?

Did your mother or father leave you and break your heart?

Or is their abuse branded on your stony heart even now?

Maybe you fell into an addiction so young you can't even remember "normal"?

Or lost someone whose absence breaks your heart.

There are twelve stories here; mine and my "Beloveds." People I have known and loved all my life. We are all related in different ways – by blood, or adoption or the "family" we made for ourselves along the way. All wounded in childhood in horrific ways. Yes, we chose other names to protect our anonymity. All the other words in this book are true and verifiable.

Maybe there are echoes of your story here as well. Stories "normal" people might see on the news and wonder if they are even true. *Yes, they are.*

Maybe your story is so dark, you cannot tell anyone, even God? You have a shell that keeps you numb, sometimes irrational. Maybe hating God for it. Maybe afraid He hates you.

This book is for all of us – us "misfits" and those who love us and want to understand us.

My qualifications for writing about it? The same ones the apostle Paul had when he got knocked off his high horse and met the Lord on the hard road to Damascus.

And Peter when he left his fishing boat to follow Jesus.

There aren't any degrees or certificates that qualify one pilgrim to help other pilgrims on a long, hard road. They do it because they survived the journey, learned a lot of things along the way. And want to share it with the others they see struggling on the trail.

And maybe it takes one to know one.

It is a "scratch" cake, not a box cake. "*Nondenominational.*" Even the *word* has seven syllables – the "number of perfection." Not one church preachin' to the other churches. Just the basic ingredients to have a relationship with God. For believers, atheists, doubters, pew-warmers and those who stalked off from Him a long time ago. Come to Him with *all* that. He knows.

I've been an active member of many churches. Like the old song that claims the singer is "a little bit country, a little bit rock and roll," I am an evangelical, catholic, charismatic, fundamentalist, scripture loving, dogged follower of Jesus. There always will be differences of traditions and customs among denominations. But there is not one point of actual *doctrine* in these pages that any one denomination should reject. Just the straight path to the one Jesus. I have my own personal beliefs and preferences, like most people. But none of them saved my life. The One who did comes to us apart from all that.

So we tell our stories, right up from the locked basements of our souls. Maybe these will help you tell God yours. Then He will set *you* on your own pilgrimage.

The Truth Will Set You Free.
But First, It Makes You Crazy.

I myself have faith and I have doubt. I love God and I hate things He allows in this world. I'm not always sure what faith should do when people hurt me, whether to cry alone or defend myself. Or worse.

He must be very patient, God. Must love with a force we cannot comprehend. Love is so much more powerful than knowledge, so irrefutable on its own. We can argue every point of doctrine and tradition in the Good Book, but would lay it all aside in a minute for a whiff of love.

This world is hard. "Fallen," scripture says. Oh yes. Very.

And surely no place for children. Dangerous, corrupted. Some of us get mommies and daddies who love us and protect us and provide for us. And some of us do not.

Really, it is the difference between us. We think it's money or fame or looks. But for most of us, it's *childhood*. Some of us were loved, safe, connected. Some were damaged in a way our bodies remember and our minds hide away in our souls.

Some of us suffer tragedies later in life that wound our souls as well. But how we handle and process them has roots in the world we experienced when we were small. We fail, we fall, we fight. There are many ways to "survive."

Everything that ever happened to us is still inside, dense and convoluted like a walnut in its shell. Young brains lay down pathways that only an older soul will try to understand. That the world is harsh, confusing, frightening. Or steady as the waves of the sea. That we are important, secure, loved. Or nothing to anyone, afraid for our very lives, hungry as trapped dogs.

Maybe that's when we decide about God, when we don't even have words. Later, when we do, they are colored by the blood or blessings of those first years. *Life is so unfair, how can there be a loving God?* Maybe we give a weak nod, afraid to rule Him out in case He *is* there. But that first idea is set in concrete.

Why would God love me? Nobody else ever did....

Let me be clear. I am not a "saint," except in the sense that scripture calls all believers "saints." I often prefer sinners. I say bad words, don't always go to church, and vent the fury of a wounded soul sometimes in a way that would impress a gangster.

5

But I also know there must be a special patron saint in Heaven lifting us misfits up to the Lord or we wouldn't still be here, would we? Many of us are on a hard journey. Or trying to love or help someone who is. The road can be steep; the laundry too ugly to air in church. Sometimes all we can do is look up. Tell our story, bare our soul. Wait for the answers we never had before.

The Bible is not whitewashed, like people think. Jesus gets pretty grubby Himself... makes mud with his spit and smears it on a blind man's eyes. Walks in the odor of his friend who has been dead for days. Touches the lepers' oozing sores.

And scripture is earthy too. *Skubala*, for example. Ancient Greek for "sh*t," no matter how it's been translated over the millennia (Philippians 3:8). Since Paul only used it once in the whole New Testament, he must have *intended* it for its shock value. And the Bible can be a very shocking book.

Everything is there: drunk naked fathers, prostitutes, beggars, liars and thieves. The Bible shows the world as it *really* is--the good, the bad, *and* the ugly. The gospel was meant for the *real* world. "Good News" for *real* people, right where they live.

It's not God who's the snob.

Maybe we have been playing both sides, hedging our bets, with an agnostic mouth, atheistic lifestyle, and deep inner longing where no one could see. But then we find other things to do with our time and our weekends, and leave it to the theologians and old Aunt Gertrude. Decide religion is for old folks, or perky people who like to sing, or the lonely, who have no better clubhouse. Decide to not decide. Get on with our lives without knowing.

Just the sort of people Jesus went to first. He spent time with rough fishermen, prostitutes, tax collectors. Shunned the hyper "religious" in favor of the downtrodden every time. He knows. He was tortured and rejected too.

He didn't deserve it either.

PSYCHOLOGY
MIGHT GIVE YOU A LABEL...

BUT ONLY GOD
WILL GIVE YOU

A NEW NAME

The Beginning:

CHILDHOOD

Chapter One

PATRON SAINT OF MISFITS

Who Are We Really?

"You better not tell nobody but God."
– Celie's abuser in "The Color Purple"

"Under the gun everyone reverts to who they are.
We may hunger to map out a new course,
but for most of us the lines have been drawn since we were five."
– "In Plain Sight" (voiceover), Season 3, USA Network

I never saw my birth mother until she was in her coffin. An uncle rounded up her abandoned kids for the funeral. I was a young mother with two babies of my own at home, but did not resist. I wanted to know the truth of the conflicting stories, memories, and imaginings about her.

A small group of strangers sat in a semicircle around an open casket, taking turns shuffling over the muddy tile floor of the shabby funeral home. They each leaned over to peer in and whisper goodbyes. So I went too.

She was wearing a pink waitress uniform and the fingernails of her crossed hands were dirty. Surprise and pity replaced both the mystical daydreams and nightmares about her.

Adopted people have a natural curiosity about their birth parents. It's partly a fairy tale hope, like we may be a stolen prince or princess. Partly it's nightmares from whispers. When I was a little girl, my adopted cousins coached me how to run away if my "real" mother ever came to take me back. My birth mother wasn't my "real" mother? Nightmares of a woman dressed in a black snake costume and bright red lipstick woke me in a cold sweat, then she shrank into a distant light on the horizon, her evil home.

To this day I think of evil when I see a single light on the dark horizon.

All I knew about the "real" one was that she abandoned me when I was two, and then I was adopted. Never saw a photo of her or a baby picture of myself. But nobody had to tell me what her life was like, as no one even dressed or manicured her dead body. It made me sad for her. Numb, stiffly aware of strangers' stares at the funeral, I was anxious to get home to my own babies. But sad for the stranger of my dreams, lying there in her pitiful flesh.

There were a few people there to whom I bore a vague resemblance... a new thing for me. I met their glances, scanning them for the blue eyes my sister had or my own tea-colored ones. I saw some of each.

Back with my own babies, I put it all away. My sense of my own identity was confused, but at the same time content with my own children looking to me for theirs. The curiosity was buried beneath the busy demands of daily life. But where there had been only blank denial before, now my mind began to fill in the blanks bit by bit.

Like most survivors, I locked away the pieces in the wordless basement of my soul, along with the secrets I vaguely remembered but did not understand, and the flashes of memories I knew enough to feel shame or fear about revealing. To this day I see it in other survivors as well. No matter how good we get at pretending, performing, a place deep within us exists that is full of secrets, fears, shame, and anger from our past, locked down in a dark basement under the house we've built above, trying to be "better than."

A study by the University of Montreal found that *half* of all childhood abuse sufferers wait at least five years before "telling." Sixteen percent of women *never* tell, as well as thirty-four percent of men.

My own memories and gathered facts were a puzzle piled in a corner, and there was no one it felt safe to talk to about them. Besides, those early memories are so dark and flickering we aren't even sure they are true. We start building *actual* memories that we *can* talk about. And walk away from the ones in the dark. By the time we are older we know we aren't quite like other people.

MISFITS. WE *ARE* ONE OR MAYBE WE *LOVE* ONE

My *actual* memories begin at age two in my new world, set in sepia like an old movie. Strangers bringing me up wooden steps, then indoors. A clear memory of my soggy diaper, chafing as I walked, heavy plastic pants holding in the irritation. Stiff leather soles on new shoes clicking on hard wood floors. I remember those white lace-up toddler shoes so clearly, tied too tight, pinching my ankles with every step.

A woman with a firm, businesslike voice patted the plastic pants covering the hot diaper heavy with burning urine: "If you go on the potty like a big girl you won't have to wear this anymore." And with a swish they went down and I was lifted up. The cool air hit my skin. Relief. Yes. So simple. I never felt their awful chafing heat again. My first memory of *relief.*

Another woman, a more musical voice, pulled white cotton panties with eyelet-lace trim out of a bag. "See? Aren't these pretty?" And held them low to the ground. Someone else helped me put my feet into the empty spaces and pulled them up.

To this day I remember the airy coolness where the hot suffering had been.

Not unlike the world as God created it, "formless and void," then light and dark.

The beginning. Everything since was set in those first forming days.

From my beginning, nightmares. Always the same. Black dogs under my bed. Being chased among huge white bathtubs set on lion claw legs. From the start it was my new Daddy who came for me in the night. Looked with his flashlight, assured me there were no black dogs. Told me stories about life aboard ship in the Merchant Marines during World War II. Showed me what brave looked like. He looked everywhere for those black dogs, left the light on, called me sweetheart. His is the only face I remember from those first days, his chipped front tooth gleaming gold when he smiled. My first memory of *safety*.

I still remember a young Hispanic woman named Vicky, their live-in maid from Mexico. My grandmother told me years later that my own toddler words were partly Spanish. So I understood Vicky. And still remember her smiling face and bit of gold gleaming from a tooth when she laughed.

A big wood-framed mirror hung on the wall behind the sofa. Vicky oiled and brushed the tuft of baby hair on top of my head into a tunnel around her finger. Then lifted me up to see, laughing. Yes! I laughed in response to her pointing finger. I saw to the other end! My first memory of *fun*.

I remember when Vicky left. From the way Mother and Daddy talked, it was a happy thing. Getting married, they said. I only knew she wasn't there and I missed her. I remember a long ride in the back seat to the rural ranch across the border into Mexico weeks later. Mother and Daddy happy and excited to go to a wedding. The small crowd of people gathered around a patio campfire outside beamed smiles at us when we pulled up and got out of the car, rushing over to shake hands and direct us to the fiery grill.

There was a baby goat, about my size, tied with a frayed piece of rope to a large truck tire. I remember reaching over to touch his fur as he bleated, tongue hanging out, eyes round and staring. Then the strangled bleats cut short by a swift knife slice to its throat. The people smiling and excited.

I know now that it was a special gesture for honored guests, butchering that baby goat to make fresh *cabrito* for the meal at the outdoor wedding. It's a common thing among the rural poor in Mexico. But the pretty evening with hanging lights and happy music was cut unforgettably short for me by the murdered baby animal. The memory of shock and stunned horror all rolled into one frame. Wordless, like the others.

Sometimes I saw bits of even more horrid memories in my mind. Younger, earlier, harder. But too young for the words yet. Like most of us, I stored them in that deep locked chest in my soul. Not clear, not safe. No way to "tell."

Maybe even the angels don't know how we got so wounded, what happened long ago to our twisted little walnut brains in their bumpy shells. We might not know ourselves. But we recognize our stories when we see them. A movie, a picture, a book. Snatches of overheard confessions. And we stop. Something sighs deep within. Our memories slide – wet, salty – down our face. Our story – dim, confusing, set in stone – never leaves us. Whether we know it or not, tell it or not.

In my thirties, I was somehow able to "see" my own story in an art gallery. The parts I knew, and the parts still lost in a dim wordless abyss.

There were several paintings that day, rich in history and color. People murmuring admiration, shoes tapping on tile floors in cavernous rooms. Art. Pictures. Stories. No one trying to *tell* them, everyone trying to *see* them. Echoes of reactions mingled in the air like faint music. Then, turning, I saw my own: Botticelli's "Primavera" the placard read.

My heart hurt as I scanned it, eyes jerking mercilessly to the dark figure on the right while I tried to drink in the triumph of love in the middle, the joy of innocence of the three figures on the left. I didn't know the mythology or art history behind it. But I recognized the Three Graces. Young women playing together on the left, pure and joyful, unmistakably erotic in their diaphanous gowns. Like young girls are. A handsome young man to their left, his sword at the ready, posing, flexing muscles, like young boys do. No mistaking Cupid at the top, arrow aimed directly at them.

To me, it was a dark dream of childhood. My own, my Beloveds. Hard to look. No words.

A beautiful woman in the middle, more mature, reigning over everything, the only figure who looks right back at you from the picture. Knowing now, like we do. Unsettling darkness to the right. A creepy male figure grasping at a voluptuous girl as she runs away. Her head turned back to him in terror, dark vegetation curling out of her mouth. When I saw that ivy I remembered things I should never have known.

Why do some children get to dance innocently together and some must run from darkness? That painting told our stories: The ugliness of our secrets, the naive innocence of our youth, and the reigning hope of love in the middle.

Later I researched the myth the painting was based on. The frightened girl is Chloris, who was in the woods when Zephyr, the wind god, found

16

and raped her. To prove to Chloris that he was sorry for the attack, Zephyr married her and renamed her "Flora," the goddess of flowers.

I wondered if young Chloris had other plans before her innocence was stolen while she was still herself and not yet Flora, named by the darkness that overwhelmed her? We miss the children we once were. Who we might have been. No way to get them back. And no one to witness. No one to tell, no one to mourn with us.

No one but God.

On the left, the young maidens dancing happily, the handsome young man guarding the garden.

But not protecting Chloris.

Life is not fair. Anything can happen.

Those of us carrying the wounds of childhood trauma know how impossible it is to build an "identity." Most of us misfits have only broken pieces of the puzzle. When we try to say or even think, "This is who I am," we come up short. Naked. Unsure.

WHY AM I LIKE THIS? WHO AM I REALLY?

When I was a young mother, a Pentecostal friend told me about asking her guardian angel its name, so I asked mine its name too. I got an impression in my mind of a very long name that I could not pronounce that started with an M....so I shortened it to Marty. It did a wonderful thing in my mind to give it a *name*. "Guardian angel" was an *idea* to me until then. In the Bible, yes, but not personal yet. *Identity*.

In Revelations, scripture tells us that when we go to heaven, God will give us a *new* name, a name written on white stone. A name only *He* knows. He *is* the only one who knows us, our "true selves." For some of us that is better news than most "normal" people could know. Our hearts yearn for the real "us" that has been lost all our lives to labels and imaginings.

"Just be yourself," they say.

If only....

Whether we tried to be who others wanted us to be or rebelled and refused to be anything others could accept, the result is the same: a false self. A tattered twist of hiding, posing, finger-flipping, selfie-taking hurt and anger and pretending.

So whatever our wounds from childhood are, it is, from the start, only God who has the answer to who we *really* are. But most of us have a lot of growing up to do before we are able to hear His answer. We stay numb, confused, and do what we have to do to survive, our "identity" a dim windowless room. I barely knew any of the jagged pieces of my own story back then. Especially those I locked away.

Children don't tell. Everybody always acts so surprised, even unbelieving, when the grown child remembers. But something in us was broken then. We paint over it with gauzy watercolors, great rolling clouds of fog.

"Did it really happen?"

"Why didn't anyone protect me?"

"Did they ever love me?"

Because we were children, we didn't know. We act out our dramas with each other. Little girls, dressed only in scarves. Chloris, soon to be Flora, trying to remember her first true name. Little boys playing bravest soldier in the world, sealed off from the heart.

"You are only as sick as your secrets," therapists say. *Yes*, we think. And still don't tell. We'd rather be sick.

Some of us hang onto shreds of grief for the tragedies that have come *since* childhood. Car wrecks, cancer, war, death comes and breaks our hearts.

Our *grief* becomes our secret. We don't want to share it with anyone, because it is all we have left of what we lost. We simply cannot lose that too.

Trauma that came while we were small causes us to grow up different from other people. Like a sapling trained into a braided shape. It survives, grows. But never looks or sways quite like the other trees.

The Three Graces from my own childhood each handled our wounds differently. My early story was mostly unremembered, drawn only in terrifying dreams, physical symptoms.

One of my Beloveds remembered hers. And capped it off forever. Numb, ready to use drugs or alcohol to keep that door slammed shut. Not to be mentioned. Ever.

Another's was wrapped in actual love, but shaming, confusing, too dark to tell. Is it love when they do things to you that are so wrong? Is it wrong to almost like it? Wrong to love them anyway?

The Three Graces we were, those of us who knew each other best – one turned in, one turned out, one closed off. Adopted and raised in different worlds. All keepers of secrets. Sick with them, each in our own way. Preserving the wounded little soul in the basement at all costs. The child who would have been someone else. If only....

The dark truths of childhood often stay hidden until later in life. A mercy of the Lord, probably. Gives us a sporting chance to build a foundation that might withstand the truth when we learn it or face it. My life caved in at the middle like a cake removed from the oven too soon. Maybe yours did too.

We only begin to *tell* our stories when it is safe. And it rarely is. For many of us, the safest thing we learned is keep it to yourself. There is a very moving account of childhood sexual abuse on YouTube in which a famous female Bible teacher tells what her own father did to ruin her life, and how the Lord redeemed it. Many of the comments below it express gratitude for her brave testimony. Yet one says she could have escaped, that *she* was just a "fornicator."

Several of us with our stories here learned not to tell people because they never looked at us the same way again. Sometimes even accused us of lying. Making it all up.

And people wonder why we never tell.

"Speak the truth in the inner being," Psalm 51 says. Like draining a swamp before planting a garden. But for most of us, there's no one safe to tell but God.

I'm telling mine, because God wants me to. Others here from my circle of Beloveds tell theirs. All twelve of us hope that telling our stories will help you tell yours as well.

And I'm telling God's story. Because He's the only one who ever came for us. The only one who ever loved us like we needed so desperately. Even when we didn't know Him or would not look Him in the face.

THE TRUTH *WILL* SET YOU FREE.
BUT FIRST IT MAKES YOU CRAZY.

"I love you," He whispers, if we ask Him. *"You are safe."* The very things we were always so desperate to hear. And we know, maybe for the first time, that we are not alone.

And we don't have to clean up first. Because He *wrote* the story. *Knows* we are not "good Christian" characters, already perfect. But unique, fascinating, damaged, beloved children. He knows the ways we are wounded are like bloody snowflakes--no two exactly alike.

Many precious souls wove threads of their stories into the tapestry of mine. Over many years, they taught me I was not the only one. Showed me what worked. And what did not. Like sparks from a bonfire, we danced among each other's lives and were gone. I love them, thank them, rejoice with some, mourn with others. Never forgotten:

Joyce, Donna, Patrick, Daisy, Leslie, Paul, Blanca, Marshall, Lewis, Martha Ann, Luis, Pam, Karen, George, Inocencia, Connie, Larry, Linda, Pat, Lisa, Nancy, James, Helen, Winifred, Lucinda, Betsy, Alberto, Mary, Tim, Morris, Alicia, Charles, Susan, John, Patricia, Robert, Elise, Steven, Emma, William,Richard, Rachel, Linda, Michael, Lucy, William, Kathy, Garrett, Sophie, Roberto, Thomas, Elisabeth, Joseph, Barbara, Maria, Billy, Theresa, Catherine, Damon, Jennifer, Charles, Jane, Michelle, Danny, Kitty, David, Alice, even Judas.... I name you and love you, like a litany of saints read in church.

And the "chosen" twelve of us here, telling our own stories for love of strangers we've never met. Life here in this fallen world tried to crush us.

But we survived.

Like the twelve that Jesus chose, all different, all Beloved. Some crushed. All for God's eternal good.

Others we loved survived too, damaged forever.

And some did not survive at all.

Other people do not know; how could they? You don't even want your own children to know. Love wouldn't. But we ache for someone to reach into the pain. And when someone loves us that much, it is a jewel in their own crown forever: *"When the Chief Shepherd appears, you will receive the crown of glory..."* 1 Peter 5:4

Love is like bits of oxygen while we are drowning. It is what we all need, what we wounded ones missed somehow. Or had perverted.

We try to be grateful for what we have, knowing that around the world there are children starving in Africa, and mothers murdered in their sleep, brothers shooting brothers. But it doesn't help much; doesn't stop that hateful inner chatter. Doesn't keep us from pulling down our lives around us, powerless over crippled emotions.

21

But maybe we are humble enough to say we don't know, hopeful enough to say *maybe*, hungry enough to say *yes*. Maybe even still childlike enough to believe, to *trust*.

What would it take to feel loved? Be at peace? Trust?

It isn't that we don't know, or that we don't like God. More like we are sure that He must not like us.

What would it take not to hate ourselves anymore? Or not to hate everything else?

The world spells relief a lot of ways: drugs, alcohol, food, beauty, money, fame, sex, smarts, and popularity. But we can never get enough. Because there isn't enough. Not anywhere.

Because we can never be smart enough, rich enough, pretty enough, high enough, strong enough to heal our souls. If nobody built it into us when we were very young, or if the unspeakable happened on our journey through this life, it is so hard to get up again.

And yet... and yet....

You know how you can see the stars in the sky so clearly on a dark country road? And how you can barely see them at all near the well-lit mall? When you know there is just *one light*, then *darkness* is the best way to find it. God *is* light; and we see Him more clearly.

Some souls are murdered in the wounding, left with gaping holes in their hearts. And there's something about that gaping hole – like those tunnels in the giant redwoods in California – that makes people *want* to drive right through them. And we are damaged a little more, maybe crushed.

Maybe, without realizing it, we invite them.

We have asked God a million teary times to heal our bodies, our minds. He has not. So, like the Fisher King, we bleed. Maybe we even blame God, not quite ready to abandon Him, but silently saying "no" to Him all the time.

We see bits of it in the movies we love.

Frodo says in "The Fellowship of the Ring": *I wish the ring had never come to me. I wish none of this had happened.*

Gandalf replies: *So do all who live to see such times. But that is not for them to decide. All we have to decide is what to do with the time that is given to us.*

Most movies and books are echoes of the one *true* story, the only myth that ever *actually* happened, the one the others grew out of. The gospel. They help us see what words fail to tell. God doesn't even speak human; He speaks God. But the stories all tell His story.

All the time we are whining and rebelling and making our own way, He is blessing us, wooing us, tripping us, even, hoping we will land – for once – on our knees. And if we do, all we can think to say is, "*Where the hell have you been?*"

Mad at the God we didn't even believe in.

OUT OF EDEN

Not even our culture of narcissism and unbelief can rob us of our stories. You can refute an argument, but not a story. "The Force" is everywhere. It is only when we dare call Him Jesus that people get nervous, back up a bit. It is too much, too strong, too hard to "believe." Posers, charlatans and television wackadoos have tried to spoil the name above all names.

Yet we want to know. We are strangers here. Misfits. Pilgrims. This world is not our home and we are not at home in it. Why is that?

Because we are from a faraway country. There is another world, one we cannot see because of the bright lights around us. Dark forces want us to believe in sparkling counterfeits so we will not find our way back home. To our true home, the one angels guard with flaming swords. The world you cannot remember, yet don't quite forget. Eden. The Kingdom of Heaven.

Where we are innocent again.

Sometimes we see it shine through the darkness in other misfits too. Abraham Lincoln was too tall and homely and uneducated for politics. John Merrick, "The Elephant Man," hid a saintly spirit in his grotesque body. Albert Einstein couldn't talk until he was four or even tie his own shoes. Martin Luther King wouldn't fight back. Winston Churchill struggled against the "black dog" of depression his entire life. People of every imaginable handicap who found a higher truth.

And all the major players in the Bible were misfits:

Adam gambled and lost everything, turned mankind's Garden into exile and suffering.

Noah drank too much and his neighbors made fun of him while he built the ridiculous boat that would save the world.

Moses had the "imposter syndrome," like most gifted leaders and artists. When God called him to lead his people he was amazed – "Who? Me?" A Hebrew raised by Egyptians. A misfit.

Abraham, Jacob, Joseph – all oddballs and wanderers and misfits. King David was descended from Rahab, a prostitute, then Ruth, a destitute widow. He was guilty of adultery. And murder. Yet his was the direct lineage for Jesus. The Bible says he was a "man after God's own heart."

The disciples were misfits. All of them uprooted from their lives to follow the Son of God. How could they have known? Why did God choose common fishermen for such a high purpose? And stun everyone by using prostitutes, tax collectors, widows, orphans and lepers in his grand plan to save mankind? Why did He use such unlikely *things* too – a burning bush, a talking donkey, dreams?

Because Jesus was a misfit too. On this earth, in the way the world judges these things.

Takes one to know one.

24

My Story

Kathy Louise

Born Kathy Louise, only flashes of early memories survive from that world. Bent venetian blinds hanging crooked in a dirty window. Newspaper on rough wood walls, daylight peeking in between boards. The long agony of night in a creaky crib on wet bedding with an empty baby bottle. Then, with morning's first light, a tiny woman with a hairnet and humped back lifting me from the soggy crib. I sensed I was too big for her, too heavy. Pity or guilt weighed me, but relief washed it away.

Then there's a darker memory preserved in nightmares for many years. Blackness mingled with flashes of horror and fear. I can still see the small room from down low, one door, no window, rusty chrome legs holding up a chipped white sink. Filthy black and white linoleum tiles, warped and sharp on my bare feet. Running. Running. So scared. Huge white bathtubs on lion's paw feet, my naked wet body slamming against the cold porcelain. Pain and fear too searing for words or reason. Buried forever, alive only in nightmares.

Then, somewhere else, cookies. Kind people holding out large flat circles of cookies beside a straw seat rocking chair: "*Vente, mamacita... Quieres galleta?*" The Spanish words a melody, staying with me in a new world to come.

When I became Kathy Jean.

Chapter Two

IN THE GARDEN

The Apple Doesn't Fall Far From the Tree

"It's wrong what they say about the past... about how you can bury it.
Because the past claws its way out."
– "The Kite Runner" by Khaled Hosseini

O nce *Upon a Time, a man woke up in a garden, naked and alone* (Genesis).

Theology aside, God really knows how to tell a story.

I could tell mine that graphically. A lot of us could. But I bet even Adam and Eve didn't tell their kids everything, once they got banned from that first garden.

Why would we even care about Adam and Eve in the Garden of Eden? Why does it matter? Wasn't that just for Sunday School?

It matters in the same way it matters what happened to *us* when *we* were young. The dark pockets you wish had been different, the grief that won't be healed. Rejection, trauma, loss. We know our souls got tricked, like Adam and Eve's did, by that snaky devil. It's hard to talk about.

The human race had a childhood too. In ways we are just beginning to see. I bet Adam and Eve were as damaged and confused as we are.

We turn away, scream in pain, and reject Him for letting it all happen. Then shut down or rebel.

You'd think God would give up, since mankind has made it plain we'd rather do it our way.

Boy, you just can't teach God anything, can you?

I wandered out into the wilderness of life about as prepared as Adam and Eve. Just better clothes. The damage from my own wounded start didn't show itself until my late twenties. Until then there were only hints. In kindergarten, when the other children went out for recess, I stayed inside, laid my head on my desk, and cried myself to sleep. At home, I often felt an inexplicable sadness. Sometimes blurting out, "I wish I was dead." To which my mother responded by making me write 500 times: "I will not say I wish I was dead."

I remember sitting hunched up and sick to my stomach with despair, watching the fat salty tears drop onto the rows of my round, childish writing: "I will not say I wish I was dead. I will not say I wish I was dead." Practically catatonic with grief and repressed anger. Learning to hate myself. Learning never to say it.

Reinforcing that crooked lesson was my father's sarcastic sanction against using "I" to begin a sentence. "Well, youuu won the gooold spitooon," he sneered when we talked about ourselves. I think he meant to make us people who thought of others instead of ourselves, which is a good thing. But for a child with a bomb in the basement, not so healthy. Nothing to do but stuff it deeper down in there. Smile. Perform. Look for relief elsewhere.

In fairness to them, they did not know about the basement. Or the bombs. They were upright, brave and strong. They gave us what they had. They gave us a lot. Very risky to take on children not your own, children damaged in ways you can't possibly imagine. In a way, all us damaged kids they adopted ruined their lives. But I'm sure the Lord has given them stars in their crowns, like He did His own mother. (Revelations 12:1)

I made it through to adulthood with little idea of what was festering in the basement of my soul. Went to college, married well. The beginnings of the life I knew I was lucky to have.

Once, a distant relative put me and my husband in touch with my biological mother's sister who lived near where we were traveling. I wanted to meet her and try to put the pieces of my early years together a bit in my mind. Find out more about the woman I had only ever met in her shabby coffin.

My aunt was a sweet and lively woman who made us feel very welcome. Affectionate, thrilled we had come, and couldn't take her eyes from my face.

"I thought you would be my little girl, you know," she opened.

No. I didn't know. She recognized the confused expression right away.

"Your mother left you with us all the time. I'm just a year younger than she was, and kept you when you she was... *away*." She was loathe to mention her sister's checkered past, speak ill of the dead.

I noticed her husband, my "uncle," circling the tiny living room. Smiling and circling. Cordial to greet us, but never spoke.

The aunt looked over at him and back at me. "We wanted to keep you. But they came and took you away...."

Her sadness was genuine. I was drawn in. Could almost imagine being loved in those first years.

"So when we had our first baby later we named her after you." Big smile.

And I admit it, I felt happy inside myself. Honored somehow. Cherished. Didn't even think to ask about the other versions of my early years I'd been given.

She showed me a picture of her daughter as an adolescent. Hair very near my color, freckles like me. Smiling. My doppelganger. The version of me who was "normal." Happy and cherished in this world.

29

Then she slowly lowered the picture and looked at me, then out the window: "When she was 21 years old she shot herself. Outside, by the pool. Dead."

All the air left that small, tidy room. The uncle quit circling and disappeared. And I went blank. Numb and blank. Again. That iron door to the basement of secrets and shame in my soul slammed shut tighter than ever.

The other "me". The one I could have been, would have been. Lost.

The rest was a wasted hour of admiring the lawn and chatting, then we left. No puzzle pulled together at all.

I made it a while longer, blessed but broken. Beautiful children, loving husband, safe home. Went back to university for a masters in English, considered going to medical school, worked, worked, worked, played, played, played, like we do when we are young.

But panic attacks became more incapacitating all the time. Couldn't stay in class long enough to finish my degree plans. Couldn't travel alone anymore. Sometimes couldn't even leave the house. There was no term for *panic disorder* back then. Only random trips to the ER for the frightening heart rate and irrational fear. Never any diagnosis, any help. I just assumed I was dying of something they couldn't figure out.

And began to seek more about the Lord I had been raised knowing somewhat in church with my parents. Read scripture more. Prayed more. Laid on my bed imagining Him outside the dappled light from a tree outside the window as I remembered doing from very young. No names or words for His presence, just an inner awareness of the safety.

I white-knuckled it for many years. When we drove our eldest off to college, waves of grief, fear and loss moved in like a thick fog. Then the panic attacks came... and stayed. Almost nonstop. I came undone. Nothing to do but go to the hospital, get tests, counseling, medication. An EEG (electroencephalogram) revealed a glitch in the brain. The type, one doctor told me, they usually see in patients who were adopted or sexually abused as a child. Duly noted. I knew I was adopted, figured that was it. No help. Always figured I had abandonment issues. That was not enough to explain everything.

In therapy, the iron door to the basement rattled, creaked a little, but held. I dabbled in revealing the secrets I knew, along with other willing patients. Tried to limp as quickly as possible back to normal, pretend everything was alright now. Soldier on. Smile. As I had been raised to do.

TEARS FALL ON THE PAGES

My faith did grow during those hard years. The faith of a wounded, desperate child dressed up as an adult. Still, it kept me hoping. Learning. Searching scripture, looking for answers. *Why am I like this?* So many questions. My Bible's pages from those years were wrinkled with my own tears.

Then, when I was more mature – "ready," I think God must have deemed me – a huge and shocking piece of the puzzle ripped that iron latch off the door to my soul's basement. Brought me closer to the *why*, and opened me even more to God's Truth. When our *own* truth is so ugly, we either *fall* or we look *up*.

An elderly relative who was there when I was abandoned and adopted decided the story needed to be told:

My birth mother abandoned me to an older man who was a pedophile. Eventually neighbors worried and called whatever child protective service there was back then. There wasn't much of a system in those days, but they picked me up and located the only relative they could find. That relative took me to the doctor.

I had gonorrhea. Yes, venereal disease in a toddler.

Those relatives could not keep me because of the disease. Their doctor said I shouldn't be around their own small children.

So I was adopted. The last piece clicked into place. I knew then why God didn't let me find out until so much later. Until I grew in Him a bit first. If He had allowed that truth in before His truth started raising me over again, my chances of overcoming it would have been slim indeed.

Now the dark nightmares and river of rage made sense.

Where was God when a pervert sexually assaulted a baby? Gave her venereal disease? Where was God when she screamed and screamed and no one came? Where was He when her mother traded her for drugs and went away? Where was He when she decided she would never be safe, never be loved? When nightmares became the rule for dreams, and not the exception?

And I saw that little girl for the first time. That was *me*. I had spent my whole life pretending someone loved me like I loved my own children.

Now one Beloveds' stories made sense too. The half-sister who had told me stories from her childhood before we got her made sense – of strange men and bottles of booze and mother leaving and men putting her on the table and doing things I had never heard of since I was removed younger.

And my recurring nightmares came clear... running running running between huge white bathtubs on claw feet. Awake panting with fear in the night, unable to fight, weary from flight. And the woman with the ruby red lips in a black snake suit, receding into the light on the horizon that always meant evil.

"My God, My God, why have You forsaken me?" Jesus cried while in agony on the cross.

"Where is your God now?!" the crowd jeered.

And for the first time I felt His pain.

It took years of studying God's Word, earnest prayer, spiritual help to process the facts. *"Why, God?"* I agonized, imprisoned by my irrational fears.

One day, I lay on my bed crying, praying. Saw a picture clearly in my mind of myself chained to a stone wall. In shackles, like medieval prisoners. My bitter, sad thoughts rose within me: "Yes! That is how it feels!" Then, "*Why?*"

Then the Lord scanned away from that image of the chained prisoner down the wall and that scene fell away. Down, down, into a dark Hell of--how can I say it?--much *worse*. He showed me what the suffering had saved me *from*. Then showed me that the shackles were how He held me, kept me safe while He healed my soul.

Yes, I have to admit it. I never cling to Him as surely when I am OK. The pain held me to a higher, holier purpose. Saved me from ending the way I began, like many do. "Pass it on" is the evil gift of so many trauma victims.

One of my Beloveds still keeps that iron door to the basement shut tight. And my adoptive brother may live out his days in prison. I forget who I am sometimes, for a bit. Just forget who I am in Christ and default to who I was. But the God who was there, who knew, who grieves, He holds my hand anyway. Helps me up anyway.

If it wasn't for the things I'd heard from my Beloveds, and seen on the evening news, I might not have believed my own story. And I do know it was the Lord's own wisdom and mercy that I not find out until I knew Him well. Would never have known *what* to believe.

The devil does like to lie.

As I write this now, so many years later, there is a story on the evening news about a pedophile who made videos of himself raping an 18-month-old baby girl tied to the bed. And these days we see posters in every public building with pictures of children lost to trafficking. Even some church websites have hard stories from individuals, many of them survivors of similar crimes. Hard to believe the things that happen to children. Horrible yet freeing to see it confirmed, irrefutable to all.

Horrible, unimaginable things happen.

God is bigger than those things.

The Truth *Will* Set You Free.
But First, It Makes You Crazy.

All of us are doomed to be children of Adam until offered the hope of being children of God. *That* is what salvation *really* means to me.

There is a home for unwed mothers near where I live, and I am friends with people who work or volunteer there. None of the girls have anywhere else to go or they wouldn't be there. Every girl they take in to the hospital is asked if they've ever been raped, molested or abused. *Every single one answers yes*. Most of them say it happened multiple times.

There are other forms of trauma that wound us in childhood. But even just this one has a toll we can hardly fathom:

According to the National Association of Adult Survivors of Child Abuse, drawing from government statistics, one in four girls and one in six boys will be sexually molested before they are eighteen years old. There are over *forty-two-million survivors of sexual abuse in America.*

Somewhere between seventy and ninety percent of sexual abuse victims never tell.

Ninety percent are abused by someone they know, love or trust.

It's an evil that only recently became acceptable to admit and talk about. One that we still have no cure for. Every other plague of childhood has a vaccination or medication or treatment or diagnostic screening device.

Not this one. Partly the shame of telling it. Partly that no one believes it. Or cares.

But there is a story so ancient, so healing, that it can transform everything. God's story begins like this:

In the beginning, God created the heavens and the earth.

My story begins like this:

I was born on a cold day to a woman who abandoned me.

And the whole human race has a childhood too. Cosmic. Archetypal. Imagine a garden so perfect you didn't even need clothes. Not too warm or too chilly. Plenty of food hanging low on the trees, animals to enjoy and tend. No awareness of any way you could lose it--no death, no enemies. No stress or performance anxiety at all. You could drink the very water you waded in. No mirrors to find fault with your perfection. Bliss. Only God to rock the cradle.

Then evil entered. Choices were made. Conflicts began. The middle of any story.

How many authors would let the characters write their own lines? Make their own choices?

Because we cannot truly *love* each other or Him...unless we are free *not* to.

Judging from the Old Testament and ancient Hebrew pictographs, story *is* God's language. It's what He speaks. You can disbelieve an idea, but there's no arguing flesh and blood. That is what a story does – gives flesh to ideas too deep for words. Shows the pockets of good and evil, the conflicts, the choices. The journey. "Show, don't tell," like the brilliant Russian writer Anton Chekhov said.

Whatever it is we think we need to make us happy, our ancient ancestors had it. And lost it. Maybe that aching regret still lives in our brains. Somehow we know how it could have been, this life. And that it's not. An ancient, prehistoric blow to the brain still causing symptoms all these generations later. Like damage in childhood echoes in the adult.

And echo it certainly does. Doctors and scientists are just now fully realizing the extent of the damage.

MODERN SCIENCE, ANCIENT SCARS

With modern scans, we can see what trauma does to brains. Subjects with childhood abuse have a hippocampus that is eighteen percent smaller than those of others who were not abused, according to a study found on the website of the National Institutes of Health's U.S. National Library of Medicine. The hippocampus is the physical "home" of the "fight or flight" response wired into our entire nervous system. Adopted and abused adults often show seizure *activity* in the brain but no seizures. There are now so many ways to actually test and see what happened. Helps us understand why we are misfits.

The largest modern study, done by the Centers for Disease Control (CDC) and Kaiser Permanente in the mid-1990s, discovered the main thing that increases the risk for seven out of ten of the main causes of death in the U.S. – Adverse Childhood Experiences, they called it, ACEs for short: violence, abuse, rejection, disaster, grief, accidents and illness.... And their scientific studies showed that these traumas are the single-largest untreated health crisis facing our nation today. A crisis on a shockingly large scale in our privileged country. And one we can only imagine how it is for the rest of the world.

This evil serpent that slithers into the garden of childhood affects at least 67 percent of us, according to those studies. ACEs cause its victims to have:

- Triple incidence of heart disease and lung cancer
- Twenty-year lower life expectancy
- Four-and-a-half times the rate of depression
- Twelve times more than the average rate of suicide, according to the book "The Body Keeps the Score: Brain, Mind, and Body in the Healing of Trauma" by Bessel van der Kolk, M.D.

Yet do we hear about this epidemic, this killer, on the evening news, like we do war and violence and car wrecks and epidemics? Movie stars and politicians?

No, we do not.

When we grow up and do bad things or seek relief in damaging ways, the world tends to think the increased risk of disease and early death are from the high-risk behaviors we seek, looking for relief with alcohol, drugs, sex, crime. But the CDC/Permanente study showed that those horrifying health statistics hold true *even if you do not engage in high-risk behavior!* The study proves that it is *the actual events themselves* that damage our brains due to stress in the fight or flight response innate to our nervous system. When the release of stress hormones is repeated over and over in childhood it changes everything. Affects brain structure, immune system, hormones, even genes.

We zigzag our way through the hurdles and landmines of everyday life stresses wondering why things are so much harder, why we are so afraid or ashamed or numb or sad or enraged.

Some of us make it.

Some of us do not.

TRUTH: FOR THE VICTIMS AND THE VILLAINS:

Like any good storyteller, our Author knows the way our understanding is shaped by our wounds. It is our *relationship* with Him that He is after, not our PhD in religion. Because He *loves* us.

Yes, I have trouble believing it too.

God begs us to leave the tattered blanket of what we know for the invisible promise of His kingdom. And if we can still walk at all, we go. Limping, wounded, half dead. Addicted, adulterous, crippled, defeated in a plethora of mad ways.

Because you have to die if you want to be born again. Die like a seed in the ground. Die to the fallen world's notion of *Self*. Choose to live in *Him*.

Or we sleepwalk through life, afraid to wake up entirely.

Or we pass the evil on.

Imagine two deep sea divers with one oxygen tank. The main diver is the source of all the oxygen; he controls it, makes sure the other diver has just the right amount. Then the other diver decides to float off on his own. Fatal move. The main diver did not kill him, but the other died as a consequence of leaving the oxygen source.

People get all kinds of wrong ideas about God, but the worst is that God is mean, just setting up hurdles and rules. It was *never* like that. God was always our only source of life and breath. And when we fatally pull away He comes after us anyway. He loves us, provides for us. Yes, even atheists. The rain, as the Bible points out, continues to fall on the just and the unjust. (Matthew 5:45)

What Adam and Eve suddenly knew when they ate the forbidden fruit of the Tree of Knowledge did not make them like God, like the lying serpent said. It made them *less* than they were before. The devil is like that. Tricky. Tempting. And wrong. The "Father of Lies," the Bible calls him. From the beginning. If you pay attention, you will see that his lies are always trying to make *God* out to be the liar.

And on it goes.

I knew a petite, pretty woman once, named Inocencia, Spanish for "innocence." I can't help but think of her now. When I met her she had two metal plates in her head, one lame leg, and impaired speech. Not a car wreck, not a force of nature. Her husband. Those of us who knew her were aghast to hear the stories – kicked from sleep onto the floor, broken spine and ribs, hands crushed in door jambs because supper wasn't right.

How many generations since Adam's weak-willed choice led to this? With people living among the stones instead of in the Garden? How long until they used those stones on each other? Adam and Eve's own son Cain murdered his brother Abel before those first animal skins had even worn out. The bloody stories are all there in the Old Testament. Right up until fragile little Inocencia was beaten to a crippled pulp by the husband of her youth. And all the sorrows in our own stories.

When I had my own children, there was no end to what I *didn't* know. But I knew I could be the end of not one but two lines of wounded, wounding mothers. My childlike faith told me I could *give* what I had never quite *received:* safe, unconditional love. And something about that really did heal the deepest part of my wound.

COVER US UP, LORD!

Think of any murder mystery you ever saw. When the victim is found naked and bloodied, what is often the first thing the responding police officer does? Covers them with a coat or blanket. That is how God was with the fallen Adam and Eve, and that is how he is with us today. That is "grace." God's unmerited favor. He covered them with animal skins. He covers us with His mercies.

I often grieve things in my background, then think of all the things God did to make it up to me. Even being willing to *die* for us like we would for our own beloved children, as Jesus did on the cross.

I went to a kids' birthday party once where they were all jumping up and down in one of those plastic bouncing castles inflated by electric fans. When the host's house suddenly lost power, the castle instantly deflated, with all the kids screaming inside. There *is* no jumpy thing without the continuous infusion of that air.

That is what happened to Adam and Eve. God made everything just for them. *He* didn't need a garden. But He wanted His beloved creatures to have it. Adam and Eve's sin changed their nature. And it changed their descendants. You got your freckles from Aunt Mathilda or someone way back there. But you got your "sinful nature" from Adam and Eve. God created us to be one kind of creature; we became another.

But God provided a red thread of salvation that is recorded throughout the Bible. All the roads led to Jesus. Through Him, all things became possible again.

But it would be a long hard trudge through the wilderness first. Which is where a lot of us still are. How to understand His love and mercy *anyway*?

I love my pet dogs, but I have to train them all the time, discipline them, chastise them, or they could not live with me here in our home. They fail me all the time, but I do not kill them or abandon them. I love them too much. I pity them. They are dependent on me for everything. But would I *die* for them? No. But I *would* die for my *children*. God created us to be His family, His *children*. He is our breath, our life. In Him we live, and move, and have our very being. Whether we acknowledge Him or not, know Him or not, thank Him or not.

We will never know *everything*. But the journey itself is a holy one. Our life's work. Putting the pieces together. Developing a relationship with the One who *does* know everything. Building our souls.

There have been other stories of gods dying and reborn, of exile and return. But *none* of them had one of their mythical gods actually *do* it – come back from the dead and reconcile men with God. *None* of them came in the flesh and claimed to *be* God.

Until Jesus.

We have our part, though. Like in the movie "The Matrix," when Morpheus explains it to Neo: *"This is your last chance. After this, there is no turning back. You take the blue pill – the story ends, you wake up in your bed and believe whatever you want to believe. You take the red pill - you stay in Wonderland and I show you how deep the rabbit-hole goes."*

And God had His part. Like in the Superman comic books and movies – a "heavenly" father sends his only son to save the earth.

Redemption has always been the story God is telling us. It is what we love in the other stories. Why we love a hero. Stories are true in a way that a newspaper article never can be. You can *argue* with a lesson, but a *story* is its *own* meaning.

Do not forfeit your soul for failure of your imagination. Things the intellect can barely fathom make the soul sing.

Take the Red Pill.

"Hey, pssst...you can be like God, ya know," the devil whispered.
And men and women, from the beginning, fell for his lies.
They already were *like God!*
And still, it wasn't enough.
The pushers and pimps and brewers and bookies
echo the same old lies,
Haven't had an original thought since the original sin.
"Pssst....hey! Take this and you'll feel like a god."
Call it "fallen," call it "sinful," call it "sick"
You know what it makes us.
Eternal Misfits.

IS YOUR HEART
BROKEN?

GOOD.
THAT'S HOW
THE LORD GETS IN

Marshall

Being adopted is confusing. Now that both of my adoptive parents are gone, I wonder about the people who gave birth to me. Wonder if there is hope I might be like my biological father and not the awful adoptive one. Wish I knew who he was, if he was alive. Wonder why my mother got rid of me. Wonder who I really am. Who I look like, act like. If they would like me.

My adoptive father was rarely there, never interested in me. A violent, perverted "big brother" melted all memories into fear. He and his friends exploring my little five-year-old body all the time, making me sit on their laps while they fondled me. Throwing me across the room, once up against a high window like a ball, shattering the glass. Then the lies to my parents. Learning to shut down and never speak truth to anyone. Not safe.

Only my mother and sister loved me and cared for me. So there were islands of love at home. But sometimes they left me home with big scary boys and once a strange man. Learning the hard way to never "tell." Not tell about waking up in my bed with no clothes on or riding in a car full of drugs and guns or where they put their painful fingers. *Shhhhhhhh* was always the message. Pain always the threat.

I can only speak now that everyone is dead or gone. Only the fear and the "why?" remain. And a faith that has learned to look up and not back. Knowing God actually loves me saves me every day. His love keeps me alive; the scars make it very painful.

Chapter Three

"Talitha, Koum"

Child, Get Up

Many of us tried to be "normal." Maybe even tried to be kind. But so many were not kind back. So we became all ears and scars, listening for cues, breaking our own hearts trying to get the love we never quite got. Determined to be the thing the world most wanted us to be: someone else.

No matter how hard we tried, we never could get anyone to say, "I love you like you are; everything is going to be alright." Until God. He was our Hero, plain and simple. Our inner longing knew we needed one.

There is a beautiful anecdote in the book *Blue Like Jazz* by Donald Miller. Navy SEALS were on a covert operation to rescue hostages in a foreign prison, but the prisoners were too scared to follow them out. Finally one Seal had an idea:

> He put down his weapon, took off his helmet, and curled up tightly next to the hostages, getting so close his body was touching some of theirs. He softened the look on his face and put his arms around them. He was trying to show them he was one of them.
>
> None of the prison guards would have done this. He stayed there for a little while until some of the hostages started to

look at him, finally meeting his eyes. The Navy SEAL whispered that they were Americans and were there to rescue them. *Will you follow us?* he said. The hero stood to his feet and one of the hostages did the same, then another, until all of them were willing to go.

Isn't that just how He saved us? Taught us to trust then follow.

When our kids were young we lived out in the country. Every Christmas Eve we rounded up all the dead branches and debris from our acreage and built a huge bonfire. Food and drinks in the house and everyone we knew invited to "come by any time." Rain or shine, by dark there were always many people circling the fire, kids playing, adults staring into the blaze, a shower of sparks swirling up to the dark night sky. Peaceful beauty surrounded by the joy of the season and relationships. A "moment" outside the hectic everyday struggle.

That fiery swirl of bonfire in the night is a perfect picture of the process we go through once we decide to give our lives to God, choose His way instead of our own crooked path.

First we gather the things we *know* need burning. The easy part. Because we *know* what is destroying us. Then we set the blaze of God's own Truth to it all like a match. Surround ourselves with others who know and care to watch the blaze.

A million kinds of bonfires, but always the same match. Life doesn't get *easy*. But it gets beautiful, meaningful. We lose the need for revenge or secrets or all the lying Band-Aids we've used, and watch the beauty of the fiery sparks swirling to heaven.

I'm never sure how God gets His thoughts into minds so twisted, but He does. The more I surrendered to His way, the more rewarding the journey. The Lord sent me an awesome Christian counselor who was gentle and patient to teach me my *true* identity... in Christ. "Holy, blameless, perfect, loved," by scriptural Truth, as said in Ephesians 1:4 and other verses. Instead of the hopeless rejected loser I thought I was. Whispered to me that I was safe. Raised me all over again "in the nurture and admonition of the Lord," like scripture says and Life had not provided until that point.

TALITHA KOUM! CHILD, GET UP

I remember the first time I read the story in the Bible of Jesus healing a little girl, Jairus' daughter

> *He took her by the hand and said to her, "Talitha koum!"*
> *(Which means, "Child, I say to you, get up!").*
> *Talitha, koum.*
> *Child, get up. Come.*
> (Mark 5:40-42)

He spoke His word to the little girl and she came back to life. She was *dead* and He spoke her back to life! She "got up and walked around," the Bible says.

"Speak to me," I told Him two thousand years later. "I am dead." And I very nearly was.

And He did. Through the Bible I devoured, through the prayers of the children He gave me, through the counsel of a Godly man, the preaching, and the singing. And through His Spirit into mine, consolations in the night.

Talitha, koum.

I got up. Began to walk. Faltering baby steps.

47

I was a slow learner. Maybe it goes in deeper that way, a slow drip. No presto renewed-o for my wounded mind. No instant healing for my body. I was alive, but I had a lot to learn.

If you confess with your mouth Jesus as Lord,
and believe in your heart that God raised Him from the dead,
you shall be saved.
(Romans 10:9)

I didn't know exactly what "saved" meant, entirely; had always assumed it meant saved from Hell. When I was too young for the words at all, I had known Him through the dappled light in windows, the merciful whispers in my soul. When older I had walked the aisle for it, but never immersed deeply in scripture and prayer. Now that I spent time every day on my knees and in the Bible and thinking about Truth instead of pain and sorrow, there were new waves of healing in my soul. And nearly every night a stunning holy dream. The one I remember most clearly was a dry cracked earth slowly being renewed by springs of clear water. Yes. Like that.

We start living *over again* when we believe. In a new way. But it is kind of like when you quit smoking. Yes, there is one day you quit, give it up, swear off. The start. The choice. But from then on you have to quit *every* day, remain faithful to your decision. Once you put your faith in Jesus, you are "in." Justified. Reconciled to God. In the "family." Then there is the daily walk.

If you love me, you will keep my commandments.
(Matthew 9:13)

At first my walk was just obedience. Trying to be a *good* child. A little girl walking about. Trying to win His approval somehow, since I had spent my life like that to just survive.

Some of us are more *rebellious*. Wondering what the "rules" are, and giving them the middle finger while we walk away... like we did with our abusers earlier. A healthier way, some say. But both ways carry their own wounds. The only cure is choosing to have an actual *love relationship* with Him. Only then do we choose to follow, to learn, to live fully.

And that is what He is really all about. Pure love. Not what we "do" or how we *perform*. Or how we *fail*, even. Nope. How we love Him back once we learn how much He loves us.

Because once we decide to do things God's way, it is like a small child's gifts to its parent. A rough crayon picture, a daisy plucked from the lawn. He does not *need* it or *require* it. But He loves it.

The only thing that counts is faith expressing itself through love"
(Galatians 5:6)

Scripture does say which choices are better. Like *we* have "rules" to keep our own beloved children *safe*. But keeping score? No. Buying our way into Heaven? No. Just our appointed mission from God, once we know Him well enough to listen.

So simple. But so hard to wrap our mind around because we are so confused and distracted by the smoke and mirrors of this fallen world:

"Be pretty," it tells us.
"Be smart."
"Make money."
"Be famous."

And like lemmings we fall in line.
Then find it is never "enough."

For those of us with wounds in our hearts, nothing would have been "enough." Admit it. Lay it down behind you. Step over it like the stumbling block it is. God Himself came down from Heaven and took on a human form to make us who we *really* are. When we wrap ourselves tightly in Him we already *are* "enough." Forever.

Yes, we have scars. But scars, in their essence, indicate healing. Hard to say it all in one sentence, one life even. But if I could, what I would say to you is this: **God loves you.** He cherishes you. Mourns with you. Stands beside you every second, breathing His own life into you. He is everything you think you've "missed" in this life. He is the only one safe to ask: *Who am I?* He is the One who knows. And He has the answer to every *"Why?"*

STILL, LIFE IS HARD

Scars heal but they do not disappear. No child grows up immediately. We wounded ones take a while to learn. Things get in our way:

- **Doubt,** of course. If God is how He says, why won't He fix me? A child's petulance.
- **Fear,** too. Afraid He will take away the acceptance we cling to. Or condemn us for our mistakes. It's hard to trust God's love when you were never able to trust anyone else's.
- **Pride,** naturally. Wanting to do things our own way. For the credit? Or performing to get love?

Still, we grow. He gives us little ways that suit only us, no one else. Who else would know all our little ways? Only our real parent. One of my ways was to say the 91st Psalm in the middle of the night while shaking and crying, putting my own name into it. Or my children's if they had a problem.

Another was to sing songs about His love, even though I can't carry a tune in a bucket. The children and I put verses of His protection on index cards taped to walls and cabinets. I could not always *feel* the love, but chose to *believe* it and live in it best I could.

He promised He was with me. I promised I wouldn't kill myself. And we walked on.

WHAT *IS* LOVE, ANYWAY?

The Hebrew word for "love" is *ahav*.... made of pictograph letters that stand for "giving" and "self." When you give of yourself to someone, that is love. Nowhere does it say it is a warm, fuzzy *feeling*. I found I could *do* what I could not *feel*. I chose to love Him by choosing His way over the other ways that come so easily. Doing it for my children helped me learn. Giving them what I had never received was healing beyond words.

The *thinking* was – and still is – the hardest part. "Renewing the mind," scripture calls it. Trying to think like God thinks instead of our default icky mess.

Have you noticed how the mind just oozes on down its self-absorbed track until you are only thinking about your bowels or what you want to buy or further down into a darker place of self-pity or lethargy? And you start thinking a drug might help or a drink or food, sex, money, entertainment. Something to make the bad feelings stop. But the bad feelings are being pumped out by your own wounded mind, replenishing the toxic supply all the time.

The flesh cries out... pain, fear, sorrow, rage. Back in the unremembered mists of childhood we screamed for help and no one came. Our souls are crimped by that unanswered cry. Yet we live. And eventually realize that a crippled child hangs onto her Father ever tighter. We don't have to wonder why He can't make us *perfect* with a quick *zap*.

Someone, something, maybe all the sin in the world, conspires to cripple us, make us unable to trust love. *That* is the sword in the stone. To learn to trust the Lord with death and loss and suffering and pain. To live a life of "yes" to Him, and not my life of white-knuckled "no's" and "oh no's" and "uh-ohs."

For all That has been, Lord – thank You. And for all that will be – yes.

That quote has been attributed to everyone from the Virgin Mary to famed Secretary-General of the United Nations Dag Hammarskjold... because it is *perfect*. And it was one of many He sprinkled into my starving soul. When that one phrase took hold in my mind, there was a new willingness to move on from the "past." Begin to imagine a God who was fashioning a soul to live forever with Him, not a cheery robot with a prestigious career, great car and nice clothes.

I was a slow, whiny student, to be sure. But He is infinitely patient. The pitiful prayers of "please, please, please" slowly stilled, and I learned to accept my circumstances. Like the apostle Paul, who learned the same hard lesson and wrote three-fourths of the New Testament:

I have learned to be content whatever the circumstances.
(Philippians 4:11)

Health was my "circumstance." "Money" might be yours. Or the death of someone you loved. Or drugs. A million things. So much peace in accepting what *is*, as from God's hand, instead of always striving for what *could be*. And the only Boot Camp training for Heaven there is in this world. It returns us, in a way, to the fellowship of Eden, walking in the cool of the evening with Him before Adam and Eve messed it up.

We never get perfect or do it every time. But now we have a true north for our inner compass.

One of the knots that had to be unsnarled for me was the "mental" part of illness. Learning that I have the "mind of Christ," just as scripture says, but how that differs from my *brain*. My brain, apparently, was a little broken. But I slowly realized that it was part of my *body*. Cannot help the crummy genes I was born with or the trauma from what was done to me. But scripture assured me I had "the *mind* of Christ," even if I sometimes had the *brain* of Frankenstein.

I slowly began to see the holy in the mundane. Mowing grass, washing dishes, taking out the trash, "small things done with great love," as the famed French saint Therese of Lisieux put it. And more time on those knees. Nothing more humbling than dirty diapers, feeding rice cereal to a squirming baby, awake all night with their fevers and vomit and tears. Never enough time, never enough money, enough sleep. Young mothers and daddies learn a lot or they leave a lot.

I doubt I would have stayed the course if I hadn't needed Him so much, all the time. On my *good* days, it wasn't His will for my life that consumed me. It was only the *rain* that drove me indoors, to His shelter.

WE HAVE OUR OWN CROSSES TO BEAR

Fear was my heaviest cross. Debilitating anxiety and panic attacks. Eventually I came to think that if fear is a problem, then fear of death is at the bottom of the well. *"Memento mori"* – always aware of our inevitable death. No amount of Christian assurance about our eternal life takes that away. Mostly we try not to think about it, think maybe an exception will be made for us. I've known people who never thought about death. I think about it many times a day. Neither way gets you any wisdom or grace.

To accept death at all, you get pretty close to trusting God. Because death really is the horror. The unknown. Yet we are promised:

> *He will wipe every tear from their eyes.*
> *There will be no more death or mourning or crying or pain,*
> *for the old order of things has passed away.*
> (Revelations 21:4)

I think how much I would have loved the beach with the children – if it hadn't been for the fear they would drown or be hit by a passing car. How much more I would have loved my husband if I hadn't been afraid I could lose him. So many beautiful moments lost to fear.

GRATITUDE ANYWAY

And at the other end of the continuum of crosses we bear? *Gratitude.*

> *Give thanks in all circumstances;*
> *for this is God's will for you in Christ Jesus.*
> (I Thessalonians 5:18)

Oh, how I wish I could have learned this *first.* I'm guessing the uphill struggles would have been shorter if I had. But it took a deep walk in all the earlier lessons to move me. To thank God for *everything.* My flesh actually flinched to hear the suggestion; a bitter root revealed itself. Give *thanks?* For *this?*

I can remember people telling me "you are a lucky, lucky girl," when they learned I was adopted. And feeling a queasy question form up in my mind before I could stop it. *Why am I so lucky? Everyone has parents, no one calls them lucky.* And ashamed of myself for thinking it. And never, never, ever saying it.

And again, the same bitter little flinch when people told me what a lucky, lucky woman I was to have such a great husband. In my mind, I knew I *was* lucky. But the bitter little child was still in there thinking her horrid little thoughts. Didn't hear anyone saying *he* was lucky.

Sometimes I think my ingratitude for His many gifts and mercies crippled me even more than the suffering did. I know people who have a *gift* for gratitude. They are a joy and inspiration. Sadly, I was not one of them. I had to learn. Still do. Saying "thank you" to the Lord is buried in the Lord's own prayer: "Thy will be done."

And I swear it drives away the demons themselves when we say it.

On May 20, 1521, a young privileged man nearly had his legs blown off by a cannonball on the battlefield. He learned the same hard lesson and puts it very well:

Take, Lord, and receive all my liberty,
my memory, my understanding,
and my entire will,
All I have and call my own. You have given all to me.
To you, Lord, I return it.
Everything is yours; do with it what you will.
Give me only your love and Your grace,
that is enough for me.
Ignatius of Loyola

He went on to live a long life of Godly wisdom and teaching that is inspirational to millions, even today, as the founder of the Jesuits. The puffed-up pride of youth and desire for honor and glory evaporated and God's own wisdom transformed his soul.

We all *choose*. But we sure don't all *succeed* every time, even when we *want* to, do we?

No. The lower goals are more well-lit and loud today, aren't they? And our wounded hearts make for limping pilgrims along this hard road.

I am constantly amazed how the damaged tangles in my brain can throw my soul off the trail so suddenly, so often, even all these years with the same choice, the same love, the same lessons. Choosing is one thing. Succeeding is another, isn't it?

Sometimes a *"screaming meemie"* of fury comes from some yet-unhealed knot in my brain or my soul and I throw it *all* from me. A child I love more than my own life does not return the devotion. A husband does not notice the pain and need. A friend rejects me for some unknown reason. Some tiny deficit in "love" bores into that deep unhealed place like a fatal bullet and I become someone I don't even know. A reminder of what my flesh was without Him. A reminder of who I still am, apart from His mercy and grace. A selfish little clot of misfit anger comes and I fan the ember into a bonfire of fresh toxins that cripple me for days.

And then He says – patient, gentle, never angry in return – *"Talitha, koum."* My little girl, get up.

And I do, shaken and ashamed, but walking again. And *thanking* Him.

He is the One who actually knows us. Knows what real love is and gives it to us. Knows about that bomb in the basement of our soul. Knows about that "get by" self we had to have to survive. Knows we hate ourselves because of it. *That* self, born into a fallen world, beaten by circumstances beyond our control is, like the world, ruined if not entirely broken. By chemicals, by trauma, by love that was crooked or absent. Only you and God know for *sure* just what happened to you or your Beloved. God knows; and His life in you is the only way to live above that misshapen foundation. Who else was ever safe to unlock the creaking door to that locked-away basement in our souls? Who else ever cared to *look*? To *ask*?

We learn this and we learn what angels envy.

How do you learn to trust God? The same way you learn to ride a bicycle.

Jesus, I trust You! I tell Him now, when the rats of worry start to gnaw.

Whether I succeed or whether I fail, whether I spend time as a sinner or time as a saint, I trust in You, surrender my life to You.

Step, step, step.

Who Are We Really?

I knew you even before you were conceived – Jeremiah 1:4-5
I chose you when I planned creation – Ephesians 1:11-12
You were not a mistake – Psalm 139:15-16
You are fearfully and wonderfully made – Psalm 139:14
I knit you together in your mother's womb – Psalm 139:13
And it is my desire to lavish my love on you – 1 John 3:1
I offer you more than your earthly father ever could – Matthew 7:11
For I am the perfect father – Matthew 5:48
For I am your provider and I meet all your needs – Matthew 6:31-33
I love you with an everlasting love – Jeremiah 31:3
If you seek me with all your heart, you will find me – Deuteronomy 4:29
When you are brokenhearted, I am close to you – Psalm 34:18

As a shepherd carries a lamb, I carry you close to my heart – Isaiah 40:11
One day I will wipe away every tear from your eyes – Revelation 21:3-4
And I'll take away all the pain you have suffered – Revelation 21:3-4
My question is – Will you be my child? – John 1:12-13

Change My Mind

I decide to change my mind;
Not humor it any more,
Or spoil it, or follow it.
But take it firmly in hand
By an act of will.
Some thoughts are dark
And tenacious as Fear,
And can only be dragged, bloody,
Back through the original wound.
Hard work.
Like wrestling an alligator.
Or an angel.
Lame, either way,
But blessed.

Elisabeth

Once upon a time, my mother and I had a relationship that many would envy. Before heroin became her first love.

Then she stopped caring much about my little stories, my questions, and my excitement for a new thing. The spark dimmed as the heroin consumed her mind, body, soul. Bits of mine went too.

When I was eight my Daddy left. Fear and insecurity shook every bone in my body. I cried uncontrollably. I just wanted to be "home." And daddy was home. Our dog. The smell of that old futon. Stale cigarettes and our laundry.

I screamed. *"I want Daddy! I want to go home!"* and my mother gave me her own remedy for numbing the pain. She fired up a joint, tears in her eyes, a bewildered look. "Here Elisabeth. Come here." In her stern voice. The nurse voice she used when bandaging a wound. She held the joint to my lips and my eyes didn't unlock from hers. I puffed like I'd seen her do. Coughed, spit. The room spinning along with my belly and brain. Don't remember much after that. Only that the fear grew much worse. Not better.

By the time she decided to detox from the heroin I was old enough to be out in my own rebellion, running from the pain. Boys, friends and whatever rebellious thing that made my heart flame with a sense of escape. "Cold turkey," she called the detox. I pictured a turkey running in circles with icicles hanging off of its neck. I was to take care of her. I suppose her assumption was that I would be delighted with this role as we would be close again. However, this cut into my new routine. My new obsession with friends and boys. "Why aren't things the way they used to be between us anymore?" she would say through watery eyes. And I didn't know. I didn't consider the years of heroin and men and this. I only considered that maybe it was my fault. That there was something wrong with *me*.

So I grudgingly began running her errands. Three AM trips to the drug store for Twizzlers and Cherry Coke. Picking up her meds three times a day. Bringing her the puke bucket at all hours of the day and night. Reading her scripture when she was shaking and afraid. Taking the occasional beatings and one memorable wild screaming episode. All on me. Taking the blame. Taking the pain. I began sleeping on the couch.

Finally she began to feel better. Decided she hated California and wanted to move to Mexico and assumed I was going to come with her. However, I had friends and boyfriends and a sense of security and I told her I was staying. She left and I cried some. Mostly because of the guilt I felt for finally feeling safe.

Mom died in Mexico. The heroin killed her.

So at twelve years old, I fired up a joint and numbed the pain. Every single day for years. Didn't make me scared anymore. And it never was a "drug" to me. More like eating a meal. Part of life. It led me into a life that numbed me, yet ensnared me. Always searching. For what?

At eighteen years old I knew. The "way." The Lord met me where I was. Yes. *Talitha Koum*, like the Bible says. *"Little girl, get up."* And He walked with me up the hard, steep, stony pilgrimage to make what I never had, give what I never got. Build the family life I longed for all along. Clinging to the Lord who lived His life in me gave me the strength and will to do it. If there is another way I have never seen it.

Chapter Four

THE LONG SAD

The Long, Hard Road Out of the Garden

Depression is the flaw in love. To be creatures who love,
we must be creatures who can despair at what we lose,
and depression is the mechanism of that despair.
– Andrew Solomon, "The Noonday Demon"

By the middle of any story, the main character knows what the problems are. The conflicts. Midway through mine I realized that "sad" was no longer an adjective in my life, but had become a noun. An immovable piece of furniture, right in the middle of my life. What had seemed like periodic blues was now a constant state of too much grief over too small a reason. "Why? What are you sad about?" they asked. Nothing. And yet....

I knew I was blessed to have been adopted by decent people. Had always been attached to my father, who modeled decency and hard work. And grateful to my mother who saw to my physical needs. But did not remember "happy," exactly. A few happy memories, with cousins and neighbor kids, a fun time for a bit – building caves, making pea shooters. But my daily life, as an only child, left with maids or dropped at preschool? I only learned how to be "good" and never how to be "happy."

In first grade, while the other kids went outside to play at recess, I used to lay my head on my desk and cry myself to sleep. At home, I scrounged candies and hid away in my room with them while I looked at books and daydreamed looking out the windows. My parents worked and left me with the maid. Alone was the norm while I was still an only child.

But by midlife I knew Who to trust with my story. God was the life preserver I clung to. There were mercies from others along the way. But meaning? Purpose? Answers? Not so much.

Once I went to an acupuncturist for a series of treatments to my crooked back. The pain had been there for years, all on my right side. On the fifth or sixth visit, he stood behind me, inserting needles and musing: "Your troubles seem to always be on the right side."

"Yes," I answered. "Nothing hurts on the left. Only the right."

Still focused on his work, he talked softly: "The oriental practitioners say the right side is the *mother* side.... How is your relationship with your mother?"

I laughed out loud. "Do you really want to know?"

The few highlights of my story were enough to make his face pale, his hands hesitant.

Bladder and pelvic pain since childhood. Can barely breathe when I'm alone. And chronic pain on right ribs, right pelvis, right knee. Nothing on the left. The body really *does* keep the score. Whether we understand it or not.

I changed churches often, learning from each one, always seeking. When we joined one fundamentalist Bible-type church there were new "rules" I had never known before. But also good teachers, kind souls. I met with the pastor to make sure exactly what those rules were.

"Can we smoke?" I asked, remembering the islands of peace on the last church's lawn.

"No Ma'am, we don't believe in smoking," the sweet young pastor smiled at me.

"Drink?" Never my weakness, but part of the cocoon of comfort sometimes.

"No Ma'am, we don't believe in drinking either." His smile a little more wistful, as if he had sympathized with people on this issue many times before.

There were others. I processed it all a bit, not sure yet. Wondering. But drawn somehow too.

"What about gum?" I teased him finally. "Is it OK if we chew gum?"

He laughed out loud. "Yes, Ma'am. You can chew all the gum you want."

"And will I need a covered dish to get into heaven?"

Laughter usually *is* the best medicine.

We learned a lot of scripture from the four-point sermons and Bible classes and had Godly people to raise our children with. Then moved on when life and circumstances changed.

Several friends were Pentecostal and I loved the exuberance in their services as well. Went to many healing services. Witnessed various examples of "gifts of the Spirit." Studied, argued, peeled scripture as we drilled down to the gold.

I learned a little more every day about how to trust God, to lean on Him, to whisper to Him in the night, listen for His love. Cried over my open Bible in the middle of the awful nights of unreasonable terror. Learned to let Him take the disgust from my blind memories, the shame from my mistakes. To love Him whether my damaged nervous system ever healed or not, trust Him when the fear and sadness would not respond to reason.

Because it doesn't take that long to learn He is always the One there at the end of every dark tunnel.

I couldn't manage a lot of things I meant to do in my life – sitting in class, appointments, commitments – because I never knew when the panic attacks would hit and I would have to "run away." No way to stay. Fight or flight, baby! And I never could fight.

My flesh was disappointed that I was never able to accomplish what I set out to do exactly, that the crimp in my brain would not let me. But the Spirit taught me a higher way.

I laid on the floor with my arms out like a supplicant in a movie and surrendered my life to Him anyway. *Use me however You want.* Went to my knees at my window at night when the attacks kept me awake… thanking, dying, surrendering. And felt the rarefied air of promise in spite of the irrational fears.

TRANSFIGURATION

God's love does for us what it did for Jesus's disciples in the Transfiguration. Read it in Matthew, Mark or Luke. Jesus takes Peter, James and John up the mountain. They are road-weary, no doubt dirty and tired. Jesus steps away from them and is changed into brilliant light, meets with Elijah and Moses, long "dead" – neither of them perfect in life – and speaks directly with God the Father. "My Son," God calls Him, and the brilliant moment between the visible and the invisible, the eternal and the temporal, is a blinding light of pure love that stuns the watching disciples. If they had any doubt before, they no longer did.

All theology aside, I love thinking about this Transfiguration. Can't say as I understand how Heaven will be, exactly. But I can picture being changed into that pure white light, all secrets, shame, regrets burned off, only peace and love and joy remaining. My "self," but perfected, loved. Not complicated, fallen love, but simple, perfect love. Nothing to earn, perform, get, do, buy, sell or manipulate. Only receive. And give.

Just like that, we will trade what Satan, the "father of lies," has done to us for the perfect innocence Jesus wraps us in. His child. Forever.

I was not able to join any groups or ministries or get another degree or start a "ministry." But He sent me children. I thought it was just "life" that motherless kids found their way into our circle. Giving *them* what I never got healed *me* in ways it is hard to explain. I loved them in a way that taught me how God loves *us*, all completely, all differently, all as we are. No way to compare the love for my own biological children to an adopted child or to an "acquired" child. Very different, each unique. I love the wounded part in one that speaks to my own wounds, the spiritual gift of "helps" in another that echoes my desire, the boldness in another that I never achieved myself. Is it the same as the love for the children born to me? In the Lord, yes. In the fields and hills of life, very different. In our stories? Wildly unique.

My point being... if you can't "join" or "minister" like others seem to do, not to worry. Just surrender. He knows where you are, how you are, and will use your life entirely – if you want Him to. What you give to others *is* what He uses as your gift to Him. We don't need the TV cameras or popular blogs or auditoriums filled with fans. We simply surrender to Him and walk in His Spirit the best we can and He brings the ways to serve. I see Beloveds modeling life without drugs to other desperate souls, babysitting for desperate mothers who have no time to seek and serve, ministering to lonely old folks in senior housing better than their families do, teaching English to immigrants in words and manners of faith, weeping with those who have lost a piece of their hearts in a hospital or disaster scene. A million ways. No spotlights. All grace.

He only waits for your "yes."

God was there when we were wounded. It is not for us to understand completely, but only to trust Him to turn it all to good for His eternal purpose:

> *...our light and momentary troubles are achieving for us*
> *an eternal glory that far outweighs them all.*
> (II Corinthians 4:17)

The one insight that helped me walk this walk the most was learning the difference between my spirit and my soul. The world talks about two parts of man: body and soul. But the Bible describes *three*: Body, Soul and Spirit:

> *May your whole* **spirit, soul and body** *be kept blameless*
> *at the coming of our Lord Jesus Christ.*
> (I Thessalonians 5:23)

> *For the word of God is alive and active.*
> *Sharper than any double-edged sword,*
> *it penetrates even to dividing soul and spirit, joints and marrow.*
> (Hebrews 4:12)

Our *soul* relates to the fallen world through our emotions and intellect... and is sometimes wounded, even crippled by that world. Our *Spirit* relates to God. He knows.

Somewhere in our unremembered past our souls were wounded. Like soldiers whose legs were wounded in the war, we limp on, with varying crutches and degrees of success. But our Spirit is safe, because it is God's Spirit living in us.

Maybe that is why some people seem more like animals than humans, if you know what I mean. That third part of being fully human – the Spirit God wants to share with us – has never been activated. It is dead. Or asleep. Just not alive in any meaningful way. They can have the charms of the soul, just like our pets do. But they are not fully human in some way we hesitate to define.

SPOTTED PUPPIES

My own animals help me grasp this rock solid truth.

I have four dogs that are like my children. I love them, but they do really bad things. They have ruined the carpet in all our houses. One ate our brand new, expensive wood shutters. Another barks at every falling leaf, and bites. One is well-behaved but smells like a dead skunk. One has to be kept separate because it is so much nicer than the other ones that they hurt her.

Understandably, my husband does *not* love them as much as I do. He pays for the new carpet, does the repairs. I don't blame him. The dogs sleep near me and we all wake up in the morning fresh. A new day. They haven't done anything yet. My husband is gone to work. Four bad dogs and me in the house. They are good company, stalking my every move. The big one helps me feel safe, because he can be a scary guy. The little one adores me with her big, round eyes. The others snuggle up to me wherever I am--happy "medicine" for that deficit of love.

Each morning, I look at their eager, happy little faces, all staring at me to set the tone for their day, see what's next. And I forget all the carpets they've ruined and doorjambs they've shredded and the barking and biting and trips to the Vet.

"I love you guys," I tell them. They wag their tails.

I think of my husband, how he is right: they do cost us a lot of money and chores and grief. I feel sorry for him. But not sorry enough to quit loving my dogs.

"You can't help it, can you?" I ask them. They prance happily in agreement. "It's because you are *dogs*. It is just your *nature*." I feel love and pity for them as well as sympathy for my long-suffering husband.

And it hits me – yes, their "dog nature." Because they are *dogs* they cannot help *behaving* like dogs. They dig, bark, bite, chew, pee and poo. Just being dogs.

And that is what *we* have, ever since Adam and Eve left the Garden. A "sinful *nature*." Human. A species that can't see God and does bad things and doesn't understand why we shouldn't. Because we *lost* those graces way back in the Garden when our ancestors believed the devil instead of God. Lost them and began to wander in the wilderness without them.

But even though I *love* my dogs, I would not *become* a dog to bring them into perfect communion with me, to become human. I just wouldn't. Think what it would cost me.

But that is exactly what God did when *we* became a self-centered, lie-believing, God-doubting species who could no longer live in the perfect communion with Him in the perfect Garden he made for us. He stayed with us through many generations of our Exile, reaching out to us, teaching us, revealing Himself to us.

I can't understand everything about God. And my dogs can't understand everything about me. But the love builds faith and trust between us. And we forgive our failures both ways.

Sure, we fail. Never perfect. Because, for us humans, just like my dogs, it is our *nature*, to do bad things. Want what we want, even though we know the rules. For us humans, it's what scripture calls our "Flesh." Wanting what *we* want all the time... instead of what *He* wants. Listening to the loud worldly lies on the TV, Internet and radio instead of His Holy Spirit within us.

But He persisted, revealing His truth to whoever would put their faith in Him. Speaking through Patriarch/Priest clan leaders, then Prophets, then Kings, leading by fire through the desert of life. And finally to the land promised all along. And then, as prophesied for hundreds of years, He came as a *man*, while remaining *God*, and offered us the chance to be a part of His family again.

SPIRIT VS. FLESH

We still have the battle between the "Spirit" and the "Flesh," the "old nature" and the "new nature," the "old man" and the "new man." Only now we have a sporting chance. Because, unlike my beloved dogs, we have a *new nature*. We are not who we once were, we are who we are *now*..."in Christ." As Galatians 2:20 reads:

> "I have been crucified with Christ; it is no longer
> I who live, but Christ who lives in me."

A "positional" truth that we can spend our lives turning into *experiential* truth – a holy walk. Sure, we still have what I call "flesh fits" sometimes. Listen to the anger from our wounds instead of the love from His Spirit and go off on a rant. But we can know the better way will still be there when we recover and *choose*.

One thing therapists of all kinds agree on – silence is *not* golden. None of the emotional pain can begin to heal until it is brought out into the light. Words. Memories. *Pictures* in our mind that tell our story. Even if we don't exactly *know* them, we *sense* them. Mental suffering –anxiety, depression, irrational moods and addictions – carries a special stigma. It's invisible, for one thing. "All in your mind." But you feel it in every cell of your body.

And for Christians, there is the tacit accusation: *if you had enough faith, you wouldn't be like that.* You can have maladies of every organ in your body and get good, regular "medical" care and prayer support. But if the organ that is slightly diseased or broken happens to be your *soul*, all bets are off. Then you have "mental" problems. Off you go to the psychologist or psychiatrist. Now you're not quite right, not quite normal. Even if they are kind about it, you can see the subtle shift when your difficulties are mental.

Is there even any such *thing* as "mental" illness? What does that *mean*, anyway?

That was the very simple and very deep truth that I had to grasp:

Your "*mind*" and your "*brain*" are two different things!

Your *mind* is the part of you that thinks, chooses, wills, evaluates. Your *brain* could have been physically damaged in childhood, it's been proven. Sometimes we can feel the bad spots in the mental road. But when we are "in Christ," we have *His* mind, the *mind of Christ*, and it is safe forever. (I Corinthians 2:16). But nowhere does it say every cell in your body is perfect. Ever.

We know who we are. And we judge ourselves, condemn our lives, try to find relief. We eat too much, or drink too much, or have too much sex of the harmful kind, buy too much stuff we don't need. So many kinds of brokenness trying to slap a Band-Aid on a hemorrhaging wound. But no. It is still there.

But so are we! We are still here. And we have moments of clarity that tell us we are still whole and human. We can receive love from others that speaks mercy to the sadness. Do things for others that bring joy. And yet, and yet....

Nothing cures it. It is the scarred damage an axe makes to the heart of a tree without quite killing it. It cannot be healed entirely. But we can still have victory; the Lord is still the answer. Let's learn once and for all that it is only a feeling; it cannot control your life unless you let it.

And it begs you to let it every day.

But we are so much more than our wounds. In soldiering on around them, we are building eternal muscles that we can only dream of now. Winning a prize better than a wounded soldier's Purple Heart. Some of the most wonderful, complex people in the world have created amazing, inspirational works around the edges of their sadness. Even Mother Theresa's diaries reveal a "dark night" in her soul in spite of her incredible worldwide works of charity.

Thousands of fragile mothers have loved their children around it, turned out strong, healthy souls into the world *anyway*. Wounded heart people generate much of the beauty and truth that sustains us in this world: the art, the music, the casserole when you're sick, the hug when you're lost and frightened. So many jewels in so many crowns.

Yet many of us will always be dealing with that wounded *brain*.

THE RIVER OF RAGE

There are things that do come from our thoughts, our inner wounded souls. Depression being the most common one.

You could make a large poster for your wall with all the names there have been for this restless sadness, from the sacred to the mundane:

- Depression
- Melancholia
- Acedia
- Ennui
- The Noonday Demon
- Despair
- The Blues
- Blahs
- Sorrow
- Vapors
- Despondency
- Malaise
- The Black Dog (Winston Churchill)

Call it what you will, I think the source is *rage*. A river of rage, over-running its banks. Why didn't they love me? Why am I like this? Why did they abandon me? Why did she hurt me instead of protect me? Why, why, why? Fury.

What can create that much rage? It is the unreasonable tantrum of a disappointed child. Or a terrorized, damaged one.

When I realized I was never going to have a mother that loved me "right," I knew there was nothing I could do about it... *except* try to *be* that right kind of mother to my *own* children. It healed that craving for me to *give* what I had never received. Any time I tried to *get* the love I needed from anyone, it always ended in disappointment. Other people *cannot* meet our need for unconditional 24/7 perfect love. Only God can do that. If we look anywhere but to Him, we *will* be disappointed.

True *joy* is a *spiritual* gift, a consequence of steps taken by faith, a will surrendered to God's. It is not the same as "happy." In the middle of great joy, the well of sadness remains untapped. We sometimes forget it is there. The devil, the world, the flesh? They never forget.

The only antidote is wrapped in loving God and others. God *is* love. He doesn't want you to love *mankind*, He wants you to love *this* particular child, *this* broken man at your car window for the third time, *this* ornery coworker. *This* one! Not one "out there." They'll come to your door if you can't get out, I swear they will. He will send them. All you have to do is love them when they come.

Never mind that you don't really love yourself.

GO TO YOUR SAFE PLACE

If you've ever been in therapy or counseling of any kind you've probably been taken on an imaginary "guided imagery" tour with your eyes closed. Most of these are prefaced, early on, with the direction to "Go to your safe place." Maybe you have a meadow or cubby or corner in your mind to go for those times. I didn't. I ran frantically to and fro, trying out the green meadows or still waters they suggested, wrapped in the warm mental blanket they suggested. Even tried staying in bed with my eyes closed. Nothing felt safe.

I didn't seem to *have* a safe place.

So much fear and anxiety and worry. So little refuge. No trust. Always holding up the ceiling with my anxiety, lest it should fall and crush us, steal away my children, my loves.

So I wept and squirmed and thought negative thoughts when a church retreat I attended once started out on that same hypnotic journey. "Oh, brother, here we go again."

But then they guided me over to Jesus Himself. "Ask Him anything you want," they said.

Really?! I thought. I could actually visualize Him sitting there, on a large rock in a wooded glen. He got up to hug me, like they suggested in the sing-song monotone. But I am not much on hugging, myself. It doesn't feel to me like it must feel to a well-loved child who was never rejected. But the idea of asking Him anything I wanted intrigued me enough to stay, let down my defenses.

And while I went through the Rolodex of worries and sorrows in my mind, thinking what to ask, He stayed with me, serene, smiling. Maybe even laughing a little bit at my childish excitement. Yes, I'm sure of it now; He tipped His holy head back and laughed a silent, gentle laugh. The kind of laugh I have when my beloved children do something wonderful in front of me. A laugh that is only a smile so full of love that it breaks the boundaries and spills over a bit.

Then they said, "He has to go now," and I imagined Him rising to leave, half turning from me. But turning back to hug me in spite of myself, smile and brush my face. I cried. *Do not leave me!* And He laughed. "As if!" And His eyes laughed as He dipped His head. "I am always with you." The answer to the question I never asked.

So then. Good to know. Jesus is my safe place.

And when I set my mind on that, I can thank Him that I am a misfit with this world.

For now, I thank Him for giving me a glimpse of His invisible goodness so I can hang on for the mission here. Thank Him for loving me even on bad days when I cannot feel His love, cannot see its fruit in my life, cannot imagine that He does, and cannot love myself. I thank Him for every cup of water, the kindness of strangers, the colors, the music, the laughter. Thank Him for the suffering that kept me close to His feet, for the ones who died too soon, the rejection that shaped my stony heart, the failures and even the shame. I just thank Him. Thank Him *anyway*.

Did you know that God saves *all* your tears? *You have taken account of my wanderings; put my tears in Your bottle* (Psalm 56:8). Only that much Love can melt that much pain and make that much glory. I often laugh and say, "I always *did* want to live on a lake."

In the Middle Ages, Julian of Norwich served God, locked inside a room of the cathedral, for the rest of her life after losing everything – children, parents, friends – to the plague. And was surer than ever that "All shall be well."

Helen Keller served God after losing her sight and her hearing. And went on to write books and become a famous speaker and public advocate for those with special needs.

All great saints of the faith rose above their circumstances to follow God. They surrendered everything to the author and finisher of their faith.

Sometimes, to those of us who have childhood wounds still bleeding through our adult facades, it seems like nothing makes any difference, even the gospel. Because our *flesh* never changes. I have very sad, scared, self-centered flesh, like I am still two years old. I do *choose* to walk in the Spirit, not my broken flesh, but I have my moments, like we all do. Failures. Is it the devil or our wounded brain chemistry? Or just the pain of walking amidst the other broken people in our world? I do not know.

But I do not *have* to know, because my life is now hidden with Christ in God.

> *For you have died and your life is hidden with Christ in God.*
> (Colossians 3:3)

> *It is Jesus in fact that you seek when you dream of happiness.*
> *He is waiting for you when nothing else you find satisfies you....*
> – Pope John Paul II

> *And then she clearly understood*
> *If He was fire, she must be wood.*
> – Leonard Cohen, "Joan of Arc"

The Middle:

WOUNDED SPIRIT, PERFECT CURE

My Story

Betsy

Daddy always did everything. Took care of mom, took care of me. I loved him, but I didn't understand what she was there for. I really didn't. She took time away from me and didn't do anything for either one of us. I heard the word "schizophrenic." Do not remember talking to her like other people. Or her talking to me. And I think I was always a little bit mad at my Daddy for letting her stay there in "our" house.

I have scars on my legs from when she tried to kill me. It was the middle of the night and I was asleep. Something woke me up—the smell of smoke or the peculiar popping noise of fire? Or maybe Daddy yelling? I could see my mother standing in the doorway, like she was admiring the work she had done. My small second-story bedroom was ablaze. I had *seen* fires before, but neve been *inside* one. It was confusing. I froze, coughing and paralyzed by fear.

Something drew me to the only window. An angel? My daddy screaming? Memories of times I'd opened it to look at the branches of the huge old oak tree? Watch the squirrels? Something. Then I was outside dropping through the branches to the ground two stories below. I can remember the curled up ball of pain and confusion lying on the ground. Tasted the dirt. Hugged my knees. Waited.

Now I'm grown up but it still happens sometimes. Fear? Anger? Stress? Some things happen and I find myself mute in that tight ball, holding my knees. Sometimes aware of people trying to get me to talk. Or just standing there looking confused when I come out of it. Doctors have words for it, but nobody has fixes for it. I don't have the heart to tell them about the fire.

Chapter Five

Love Deficit Disorder

The Diagnosis

Most of all, love each other as if your life depended on it.
Love makes up for practically anything.
(1 Peter 4:8)

"All you can bring is love." Kitty Smither, live from Heaven

If I were a world-famous psychiatrist, the label I would give most of us wounded ones is this: ***Love Deficit Disorder***. We did not get what even the flowers need...love and care. Or got it in a way that damaged us in the process. Or too late. Or crimped a bit by someone who loved us in their own wounded way.

The world thinks up labels and diagnosis terms that do not help: neurotic, depressed, anxious, Dissociative Identity Disorder, sociopath, Borderline Personality Disorder. So, all of us wounded people—you, me, someone you love but do not understand—start to think we are just "bad." That it is all our fault and there isn't a "cure." Pills maybe. But no solutions.

Each of my own twelve Beloveds whose stories are set between these pages has a different story. All wounded in ways our conscious minds may or may not recall. None of us found exactly what we hoped for in this world.

But our merciful Lord did find ways to show us, teach us, and pull us to Himself. Even when He had to knock us down to our knees first.

Years ago, I began writing a story for a novel. There was no intention of memoir or facts in my mind at all. Just wanted to make a connection to the main character's infancy, with a strong mental image coming to mind. So I began:

> *The baby rolled against the cold slats in the crib, her stomach a hard knot of hunger. The cold and wet and fear held her tightly.*
>
> *She cried out into the darkness; it did not answer back. She fell, but no loving arms opened to receive her. Fat, hot tears rolled down and her nose filled. Hard to breathe and cry and stay warm. The long, dark night surrounded her.*
>
> *The silken strand of safety and trust was lost forever.*

With those first words I was crying uncontrollably. Blindsided, I felt it in my body even while my mind resisted. My mind's eye could see the dim hope of early daylight, then the dark figure of a tiny woman leaning over the crib. Then a sense inside me that I was too large for her. I put my arms around her neck. Knew she struggled under the weight but cooed softly to me anyway, comforting me. I could feel a hump on her soft back, smell the dampness of her hair, gathered inside a net.

And knew, as I wrote the words, that it was all true. Memories. Not fiction. Actual sensory memories from a time before I had any words.

I asked my half-sister, two years older than me, if there was a tiny woman with a hump on her back in those days, one who wore a hairnet and could have been there. She didn't hesitate a minute. "Yes! Mrs. Bedman! She took care of us sometimes." A kindly neighbor lady, apparently, who knew our circumstances well enough to check on us sometimes. That is all I know about Mrs. Bedman, other than I will look for her tiny blessed self when I get to Heaven. My brain and soul stored her mercy forever. Even while my soul lost the ability to live with trust instead of fear.

Our childhood is more about what we *sensed*--smelled, felt, heard, saw, tasted--than words or understanding. No one could ever *explain* all that to a baby, could they? But it was stored deep within, impossible to expunge, forever leaping out in similar circumstances. To this day, I am afraid of being entirely alone...illogical, irremediable. Not a social desire, or an outgoing personality. Just an embedded fear: "What if no one ever comes for me?"

So many of us have that lost echo of mothers we have lost, trust we had broken. Just in my twelve Beloveds:

Daisy's mother hid in a back room while her father violated everything in her, ruined her ability to ever understand real love or normal sex or deep soul truths. Her fury was always at the mother who did not rescue her, not the father who ruined her.

David lost his mother in a fiery car crash when he was nine and reenacted the abuse and trauma of his childhood the rest of his life. He never knew what "normal" was and spent most of his life in prison for it. Never a dangerous soul, just a damaged one.

Betsy lost her mother to mental illness and the fire she set trying to burn her down in her own bedroom. When I knew her, a mere look or a word could send her into a tight fetal position, unreachable for hours.

Patricia remembers holding her mother's hand when she was five years old, then looking up at her mother's boyfriend as he shot her dead beside her.

Michelle lost her mother after her baby brother died in her lap when she was only four, alone, no one to call.

Elisabeth didn't lose her mother until she was old enough to survive intact and bold...except for the addictions that mirrored her mother's own.

And some of us never knew the normal love of a father. Whether by violence or absence or perversion or scorn.

And Marshall's was a combination of scorn and perversion and absence that marred his soul.

Our own "Judas" was a hardened copy of his own father as well.

It's people that broke us. And it's people who shake us now. Takes a misfit a long time to see it's not what *we* did wrong entirely. Just what we did to ease the pain, not be alone, and numb our souls.

And confusing. Because there aren't always clear villains or heroes. The good is clouded and mixed with the bad. The love with the rejection. The pity with the scorn.

I remember my adoptive Daddy's freckled back, holding me up safe in swimming pools or the ocean. Teaching me what safety was, how laughter could join the fears. Loved? I think so. Perfectly? No. Not like I've loved my own children. But he gave me what he had. Made me stronger than I would have been.

And my adoptive mother, not really the one who wanted us. She wanted children of her "own." I read it in her own handwriting in her travel diary. They both wanted their own children, not somebody else's mistakes. I can't blame them.

And one dear young man who had to live on the streets on drugs to avoid his own toxic father's constant berating.

Probably for most of us misfits, there are confusing shadows--mothers and sick uncles and sadistic cousins and neighbors...most of them victims themselves. Of poverty, ignorance, violence...their own wounded beginnings.

Who to blame? *Their* mother? Alcoholic father? Violently sadistic incest? All the way back to Adam and Eve.

86

EVERYTHING LIES IN THAT FIRST GARDEN.

Ours and the human race's.

Even riskier to *marry* someone wounded like that. Anyone who tries will need really big medicine, and lots of it. Trust me on this. Only God's love is big enough to cover all this damage. Better you know and reach for it more than most. Because you cannot understand the things your soul never suffered. But you can love them anyway, in His pure way.

Revenge does not heal either. There is some comfort in the promise that special judgment awaits those who stole our innocence:

> *"And whoever welcomes a little child like this in my name welcomes me. But if anyone causes one of these little ones who believe in me to sin, it would be better for him to have a large millstone hung around his neck and to be drowned in the depths of the sea.* (Matthew 18:5-6)

But justice, even God's own revenge, does not heal a soul either.

I ask the Lord Himself sometimes, "Why *did* You make me, Lord?"

"To love and be loved," He tells me.

Yes. That is what we all want. Even God. Maybe that is how we are made "in His image." And that is what so many of us missed. And crave. That is what scripture means when it says God *is* love and that He *saves* us. And why nothing else really can.

Takes a while to learn that *real* love is *not* a *feeling*. No. It is much more than those fleshy tickles and hugs that come and go. Takes us a while to learn the difference. God's love is not *emotional*. It is what we *do*. And *don't* do. First Corinthians in the Bible is always called the "love chapter" and it starts our education in that department:

"Love is patient, love is kind and is not jealous; love does not brag and is not arrogant, does not act unbecomingly; it does not seek its own, is not provoked, does not take into account a wrong suffered, does not rejoice in unrighteousness, but rejoices with the truth; bears all things, believes all things, hopes all things, endures all things."

So, more about how we *act*, what we *do*, than what we *feel*. More what we *choose* and tolerate in His name. And the Holy Spirit is its boss, that's all I've nailed for sure. Since we know God IS love—pure love—anything we do according to His Word in scripture, His leading through the Sprit? THAT must be real love.

Some of us have never been to church or had anyone of faith to talk these issues over with. Some hear a bit here and there, but the confusion grows. And some of us have been around Christian talk our whole lives and still don't quite get it. Sometimes it was more like "church talk" and not a straight-up Jesus relationship.

Maybe we even surrendered our lives to Jesus best we understood, yet know we are missing something. We go to church and absorb a little or a lot; some like a sponge, or maybe only wood. Some like flint, not absorbing it at all, resisting it even when surrounded by it. For a lot of reasons.

But God's grace—His "unmerited favor"— does have a way of seeping in, even in very hard places. Like music. Or books. Or even a movie sometimes. He comes to us. Tames us, like an animal, one patient bit at a time. Sits with food for our souls in His outstretched hand. We take the food, the blessings, sit a little closer every day. Learn what love is. Then—longer, harder road—learn to trust it.

We want so much to be known and loved for who we truly are. Especially those of us who have not found a good fit within the world. *No one sees me,* *no one knows...*We are hungry for someone who loves us, who "gets" us. Yet what is more terrifying than revealing our true self? We have spent so much of our lives hiding our secrets in that convoluted walnut shell. Or protecting ourselves from the labels the world is eager to put on us.

That is the simple beauty and power of the gospel: we find out who we *really* are by discovering who the creator of the universe *says* we are. *Him* we might believe. *His* love never shames us. Sure, there are iffy churches and broken preachers and fleshy believers out there, many ways to become confused instead of heartened. But when we look *up* not *out, then* get on our knees instead of our high horse, He does find a way to get His Truth to us. If there is no *love* within those songs and dreams and bits of conversation you hear, move on. Because that is what He is. Plain and simple. Love.

In the world, it's hard to get love to come out *even.* I love some people more than they love me. And know some who love me more than I love them. Those we love die before their time and leave a hole in our hearts. And we crave the love of some who do not seem to have it to give. It's confusing, disheartening.

Unless God really *is* Love, just like scripture says:

*The one who does not love does not know God, for **God is love**.*
(I John 4)

Then we begin to see that "love" is not a *feeling,* but a bedrock desire for the good of the other person. A dim reflection of God's perfect love for us.

We are not scientists, most of us, and can barely comprehend the elements at play in their theories. But I wonder, if God *is* love and *is* the Creator and energizer of the universe, then we are all truly inside the exploding, ever-expanding sphere of His fierce love. And, in the exchange of energies at *this* level, maybe it won't matter how much love we *got,* but only how much we *gave*. Because even if it is too late for you to *get* the love you missed, it is never too late to *give* it.

We participate in the most powerful force of the universe when we give that cup of cool water in love. The rest is up to Him. If it's all you can do, *love* is eternally "enough." Just do that today, and He will say "Well done, thou good and faithful servant." That is the real "secret" the world is forever chasing. How to *truly* "be somebody." Not the sad little sequined celebrities and politicians media tries to tell us are "somebody"...right up until they hang themselves in their closets. But the beloved child of the creator of the universe.

The meaning of Life, then, is wrapped somehow in the mystery of Love. Why else would any of us ever have kids and love them so much we would *die* for them? They want want want and need need need and exhaust us with their illnesses and expenses and moods and fits and poop in their pants and pee on the floor and write on the walls and don't listen and don't mind and do everything you can imagine to kill love. Yet still we love them, and, yes, would die for them. They are the only thing that can break our hearts forever and we will still weep to have them break it again.

If that is all you can understand about God, then, it is enough. "God is love." When you care more about the needs of someone else than you do about your own. When you want His best for someone, whether they know enough to want it for themselves or not. Whether they love you back or not.

Love really is the most powerful force in the universe.

But most of us spend our lives looking for the *next* most powerful force in the universe. To quote Pascal again: "Evil is easy, and has infinite forms." But giving love feels almost like getting love. Healing. Holy. Giving money doesn't feel like getting money. Giving time doesn't feel like getting time.

Only love.

The Leonard Cohen song "Anthem" says it well:

The birds sang at the break of day
Start again I heard them say
Don't dwell on what has passed away
Or what is yet to be
...Ring the bells that still can ring
Forget your perfect offering
There is a crack in everything
That's how the light gets in
There is a crack in everything,
That's how the light gets in."

A broken vessel of fragile clay lets in a lot of light.

GIVE WHAT YOU NEVER GOT AND BE HEALED

So I think we should call our soul-sickness "Love Deficit Disorder." Burn the DSM V manual the shrinks use and get real. If we loved God and others more than ourselves and they loved us back the same way...*voila!* Cured. That is "perfect love."

Remember the Bible story about Jonah and the whale? Not a children's story, like you'd think. God told Jonah to go prophesy to the citizens of Nineveh, tell them they must repent of their evil ways or He would judge them.

Jonah did *not* want to do that. He couldn't *stand* the Ninevites and did not want to share the Lord's mercy with them. He went in the exact opposite direction. And was swallowed by a huge sea creature, where he stayed for three day. Then he was barfed up onto the beach at Nineveh. Hey, God has His ways! *Then* he prophesied to them! Oh, yes, he did.

I know how Jonah felt. I had been mad at my adoptive mother for years when she became ill. Had become, over the years, a dutiful daughter instead of a loving one. We did right by each other, but missed the mark over and over. I was just not her kind of person and she was not mine. She was wounded in her own way. And I had a very long tail, easy to step on. We wanted something from each other that neither one could give. Sometimes I prayed and asked the Lord to arrange things where I would never have to see her again. He promised me Heaven was a large place.

The Lord wanted me to share His goodness with her. His love. And her a cranky citizen of Nineveh. I did *not* want to do it. So I was in a very dark place, just like reluctant Jonah. Camped out there in the dark belly of a whale.

Until she became terminally ill.

Then my will changed slowly, grudgingly, like a huge, rusty iron door, creaking and protesting. But it did change. I willed myself to read scriptures to her, share loving stories with her, care for her best I could, in spite of my dread of rejection. Like Jonah, I learned I could not always *feel* love, but I could always choose to *do* love.

There at the end, there was no one to take care of her but me. And there was enough love underneath the mudslide of anger to compel me to do that. We hunkered down into grueling weeks of medical intervention and despair and comfort and peace and panic.

Then, towards the end, she was the brave one. She went first. She struggled to raise herself from her hospital bed, pushed away the oxygen and debris of critical care. Barely able to breathe, whispering for days now because her voice was gone, she cleared her raspy throat and spoke my name loudly, a hoarse shout. It shocked me and I turned to her, came to her side.

"I love you to the end of the earth," she whispered. She had to garner every ounce of strength to say it, to make her voice project past the illness.

My heart broke.

"Ohhhh," I said back, in instant tears. "I love you to the end of the earth too." Everything else disappeared. Everything. And the night she died, in the dim light of the open closet, I saw a cloak of wings, like angel wings never worn.

Now she is gone from this life forever. Not that long ago, I hoped I would never have to see her again. Now I talk to her every day. I love her just like she always wanted to be loved. And she is tender and gentle with me, like I always wished she would be. It is a miracle that breaks my heart over and over again.

Now I have a confidence that I did not have before. That God will do that for me, with my children, with my neighbor. Even if I fail Him, and them. Only love will survive His scorching justice and mercy. Only love. As for the rest, a fleeting spark, like burning hay. Wave after wave of perfect love, forever expanding outward, without end. The ways I disappointed my parents, my friends, myself.....pffft......gone forever. In its place only the shining kernel of love that was underneath it all.

Our grief will be the price we paid for love.

The senses—sight, sound, smell, touch, taste—were made for *this* world. God's Holy Spirit, sent after Jesus left this world for the last time, is how we know Him now. Trust Him to teach you, talk to you. Learn to hear with your *spiritual* ears. All you have to do is *want* to; He will do the rest. Because He knows: love hurts and love heals.

And all you can bring, when it is all finished, *is* love.

Apologetics

If I was your mother or your father in this world,
I would have loved you more than anything.

My touch safe and tender,

you would never have wondered if it was right or wrong.

You would never have learned shame.

I would not have spoken to you through a haze of alcohol or drugs.

And I would never have left you alone.

I would have used my words and arms and food

and smiles and gifts to tell you how special you were.

I would have brushed your hair so gently, whispering my love.

When you cried, I would have held you,

I would have believed *you* and not *them*, preferred your company to theirs.

Because I wasn't your mother or your father in this world,

it is too late for some things.

All you can do now is surrender.

Lie back in my arms. Say this:

Thy Kingdome come. Thy Will be done.

I cried when they wounded you.

And carried you over more places of ruin than you see.

How old were you when they hurt you?

That is how old you are in your wounded soul.

Let me speak to your soul like a child.

Because I love you more than the stars and moon and flowers,

more than waterfalls and mountains.

You are safe with Me; let me hold you. Sh shh shhh.

I will speak to your heart in the silence:

I *made* you. It is no accident you are here.

You are here because I love you and want you to love me back.

So simple. Yet so hard.

But you are a hero!

Look how the journey has made you strong and clever!

Maybe you need to forgive them now, precious baby.

Maybe you need to forgive Me too.

Because I could not save you from them without stealing their souls,

turning all of you into hollow shells.

Your journey is only now beginning. Forever is a long time, my child.

Your real life is before you.

Because you are my child now.

--God

GIVE
WHAT YOU NEVER
GOT
AND BE
HEALED

Michelle

When I was four I got to pick a new name so the bad guys couldn't find us. I picked Michelle. I was scared when we slept in empty rooms and under trees. I liked the old trailer better, but the bad guys always came on their motorcycles and then one stayed and hurt us all the time. Butch. He got me a new white bike with a white wicker basket with a pink daisy on front and training wheels. But I was scared of it. In my nightmares it had teeth and would chase me and eat me. I never rode it.

One time Butch hit me so mother put me in the closet again. I could hear him yelling and hitting her. She took him outside and left with him, but ran back inside to yell to me "go next door if you need anything."

After it was quiet a while I came out of the closet. My baby brother was playing on a mattress on the floor. I sat on an orange rug beside him. I remember the air vents on the floor, blowing dirt in the air when it turned on. It was dark outside then and the baby laid down beside me and slept.

After a while, I remember he didn't seem right, was too still. He was too heavy for me to lift, but I moved him over and stood up. No one else was home, I didn't know what to do. Plastic GI Joes on the floor hurt my bare feet, but I limped over by the sofa. I remember burping up a taste like rotten eggs.

My mother and Butch came back and walked over to where the baby was laying on the mattress. They started screaming *"What did you do??!* The night went dark and our lives were never the same again.

I stayed with strangers and was lifted in and out of cars. Never saw that trailer again. Never saw my mother again. Never saw my baby brother again. Someone—my grandma?—told me he was dead. I couldn't feel anything. Wasn't sure what it meant. I know now. Never sure if that hole in my heart is for him or for my mother. Or for the scream that haunts me: "*What did you do?!*" Grown now, I know he died of a birth defect in his heart. But the fear and sadness made a defect in my own heart.

CALL ME ISHMAEL, TOO

Rejection: The Deepest Wound

Nobody has ever measured, even the poets, how much a heart can hold.
--Zelda Fitzgerald

Once there was an elderly man and his wife who had been good God-fearing people all of their lives. They wanted children, a family of their own, so bad. But it never happened. When he was 100 years old, deep in prayer, the old man felt in his spirit that God told him they were going to have a son. He laughed out loud and shook his head. His wife was 90 years old! And him 100! That could never happen!

So the old couple thought they would help God's plan along (like we do) and decided to get a child another way. The wife found a young woman willing to bear a child for them. A surrogate. Yes, they thought. That would work. She even let her elderly husband have relations with the young woman, and they were both happy when the young woman conceived and a son was born. They all happily raised the baby together.

Then, miracle of miracles, the old woman *did* conceive her own natural child! And a baby boy was born to the elderly couple, just like God had tried to tell them all along. And then they understood and believed God's whispered promise.

So then they kicked out the young woman and her boy who they had been raising as their own.

Screeeeeechhhh..........

Whaaat?!?!!?!

They just kicked them OUT?!?!

OMG.

And that, in case you haven't snapped to it by now, is the ancient story of Abraham and Sarah, and Abraham's son Ishmael by Hagar the handmaid/surrogate. Right out of the Bible. Another Old Testament story we have yet to fully fathom.

We get that God's promise to Abraham and Sara was fulfilled...they did have a natural son, Isaac, who would inherit all God's promises. And the Bible tells the rest of the story of that special covenant.

But my heart always sinks a bit when I read it. I feel an inner pain as Hagar and Ishmael trudge away from the only home they've known, out into the desert.

But what about Ishmael? I always think.

Poor Ishmael—he didn't ask to be born. He lost his birthright when the "real" son came along. I've always felt *sorry* for him.

Even God foretold: "He will be a wild donkey of a man; his hand will be against everyone and everyone's hand against him, and he will live in hostility toward all his brothers." Another story right there! A story for another day.

Rejection was the stone dropped on many of us early in life too. This stone is heavy. And it never goes away. Because the world provides infinite opportunities for more of the same. Ripples of rejection fan out from every unkind remark, loss, failure.

We must all be born needing love, because when that gets crimped along the way, it changes us for life. Like we are born on Life Support, and as long as it is on we prosper. When they leave or turn it off or down....pffft. Damage.

Yet it happens all the time in our fallen world. Your mother or father abandons you or they stay and treat you wrong...abusing, belittling you. Or they divorce and confuse everything. Or they die in a car wreck and you never see them again. A child's mind doesn't know the difference between intentional and accidental rejection and abandonment. Their brain will grow around that wound best it can, but will always bleed a bit.

You see it everywhere in nature. Young trees are braided or trained in odd shapes to sell as curiosities. Damage to a fingernail bed causes that nail to grow out a little warped. Once I saw a huge walnut tree that had grown up from a seed through an old wood and iron wagon wheel. That old wheel was at the literal *heart* of that old tree, imbedded forever. You could *see* it, but it could *never* be removed. Some pioneer heading West in the 1800's dropped some walnuts at that fertile spot by a creek where they changed an iron wheel, never imagining that the abandoned wheel would shape the tree that would grow there over the next 200 years.

WHAT DO WE DO WITH IT?

Most people think sex, drugs, and rock n roll are the main dangers to our youth. Not so. A 2001 Surgeon General report said that *rejection* is a greater risk for adolescent violence than drugs, abuse, gangs, poverty...anything that society tends to blame it on. School shooters and people who "go postal" in the workplace are almost always found to have suffered a recent dose of *rejection*. (https://www.ncbi.nlm.nih.gov/pubmed/20669522).

Most turn that pain elicited by rejection *inward*...where it causes the "mental" illnesses so prevalent today: depression, anxiety, suicide.

Special fMRI (functional magnetic resonance imaging) studies show that rejection stimulates the same areas of the brain as *physical* pain. Even worse--emotional pain from rejection is more *permanent* than physical pain. Studies confirm that we remember every dose of rejection, while the pain from broken bones, skinned knees and sprained ankles fade over time.

I have to confess I have failed in resolving it entirely. I know, and love, and have had my very *life* saved by God's love. But deep inside, where I am still a wounded two year old, the bloody place from that oldest wound waits and scans for a whiff...even goes to the light of potential rejection like a moth to a flame. Moths don't know that we will find them in that hot lamp later, dead and desiccated. And rejected people do tend to lay themselves out there for insensitive others to make fresh tracks on them. Or they keep themselves numb, even while their life falls down around them.

When I was younger, a good dose of rejection could keep me in bed weeping for days. Weeks sometimes, if it was my parents who rejected me. As I learned more about God's truth and my identity in Him, I could get it processed in days. Then a couple days. Now I can sometimes turn it around in less than 24 hours if I spend some time before the Lord with it.

The only antidote to *rejection* is *acceptance*. And only the Lord Himself has doses big enough to heal our heart. It doesn't make the bruises hurt less right away. Mine never do. But only the Lord and a very few souls with skin on 'em ever could. Or ever tried.

Studying, meditating, and absorbing His acceptance takes time. Sometimes it comforts me while I suffer to think how much *He* was rejected. Jesus! Over and over again. When He read the Word to them in the synagogue, it enraged them. As Luke 4:28-30 tells us, they tried to throw Him off a cliff for telling them a hard Truth.

So somehow it cheers me that I'm not the only one.

If we could *see* the effects of rejection, we would have huge government grants to study it and help its victims before they become violent shooters or closed off depressives. But it is *invisible*. Hidden. Buried beneath our masks and brave fronts, covered over by denial, addictions, rebellion, and depression. Medicine might help mask it, and counseling help unmask it.

But you can't unbake a cake.

Some become clingy, needy people; some become rebellious narcissists with a sense of entitlement. Some stay home and hope nobody hurts them again. Some go out and are brave but broken, looking for drugs or alcohol or sex or shoes or jewelry or food or *something* to take the edge off.

Rejection is probably the source of most of the Jerry Springer mode of family relations. Hurt, reject, get even, alienate, isolate, abandon, abuse, neglect. Then reload and do it all again. To this day, when people step on my admittedly long tail I go into a tailspin for a while, crying from that unre-membered place. Something inside me remembers the birth mother who abandoned me, the dark strangers who abused me.

Knowing all this by itself is not enough to heal our brains. And the crutches and escapes we find for ourselves usually do more harm than good. There just isn't anything but God with medicine *this* big. The more you make a straight pathway in your brain with His truth about His love for you, his acceptance, the more it fills in the deep and crooked grooves of those childhood wounds. His name really is above all names, just like Philippians 2:9 says. Above the labels the doctors put on you, above the names you call yourself, above the names they call you. That is how He heals you, even if you still live with an iron wagon wheel embedded in your heart like that old walnut tree.

I got rescued younger than some. But a large part of my soul is forever two. All of my life I have been more sad than the other children, more anx-ious. But children do not have a language for that sort of melancholy. I was also grateful to my adoptive parents and my childish notion of God for my life. Because by the time we adopted my half-sister, when I was ten and she was eleven, I knew I had been fortunate to escape. She had vivid words, recent memories, for the same dark things I barely remembered except in dreams and mental images.

NOT JUST SURVIVAL

The devil spins the web of vile perversions relentlessly. It is easy to see how the whole world fell with that one sin of Adam and Eve. One drunk ruins five children who grow up to be criminals and addicts. One sex addict infects a dozen girls with the poison of perverted love. And all of these grow up to be scarred, toxic mothers and fathers themselves. *Unless they reach through the web to the Lord.* He stands ready to redeem, convert, transform.

But oh, baby, you better believe the Devil is trying to ruin that idea these days! Making fun of "church" or "religiosity" all the time, everywhere you look, especially on TV. You have to be braver than ever, and reach through that web of lies to the only One who can fix what broke in you.

In my mind, what we're going for in this hard life is "holy," not just *survival*. Not just pleasure as opposed to pain. Because we *could* just take drugs. Lord knows they are easy to get. We *could* eat bonbons and watch television all day, never go out. It would be easier. But if suffering means *anything*, if there is *any* reason one person gets to be affluent, easy in his own skin, and another is poor and tortured, then it must be about "forever." And I want, with everything in me, for "forever" to be "holy." Safe with the God who saved me. I have tried psychology and doctors and medicine and food. But not until the Lord Himself whispered to me did I start to heal.

THE PERFORMANCE OF A LIFETIME—AKA "PEOPLE PLEASERS"

There are, for the most part, two ways people go with that extra rejection baggage from childhood: Performing or Rebelling. People Pleasers vs Rebels.

Those of us who folded up and went under learned to tap dance, "perform", mind our P's and Q's, hoping no one would reject us again. Most people's love is at least a little conditional. I watched as my adoptive mother rejected other adopted siblings for their poor performance, and tried to up the ante on my own. I tapped and tapped, whatever dance was called for. Never misbehave or answer back. Do well in school. Smile all the time. Here is what I learned about trying to win love with your performance: *It doesn't work.*

Nope. Nothing works to *get* love from others. And therein lies the rub: That is what most people misunderstand about *God*. They think He's like their parents and is withholding His love, pending their *performance*.

No, no, Grasshopper. If you don't deeply consider anything *else* in these scratchings, consider the *unconditional love of God*. The more you read the Bible, the more you see what heinous sinners He loved and used. He called King David—an adulterer and murderer--"a man after God's own heart" and made a covenant with him that resulted in the salvation of the *world*.

Rejection can make us feel we're loved for what we *do* rather than who we *are*. And no amount of achievement is ever enough to satisfy it. In case you ever wondered why some beautiful, rich, famous people kill themselves. It is never "enough".

Once I asked my husband to pray for me; I needed a good answer from the Lord about a recent dose of rejection from someone. I did not know how to handle it, what to do. I am deeply allergic to rejection; my instinct

107

is to never talk to them again. But I also know God wants me to love them, forgive them. The pain makes it hard.

Sometime later, my husband came with the Lord's answer. He lacked words to describe it, squirmed around a bit.

"So, did He tell you anything for me?" I asked him.

"Yes. Yes, He did. Just hard to describe." He was obviously uncomfortable with the answer.

"Just tell me."

"Well, He says to just walk around the turd in the grass."

I laughed out loud. And wept for joy to have a God who knows me so well and a husband humble enough to deliver a message that embarrassed him, made no sense to him. Because that was the perfect answer to my dilemma. I love these people, but they hurt me so often. What to do? I understood perfectly. Love them; ignore the fresh turd they left in the grass of our relationship. Step around it. Do not pick it up, try to "fix" it. Do not run away from it. Just walk around it. And move on. No, I can't always do it. Haven't achieved perfection yet. But yes, always a grace when I can.

Think of it next time (there *will* be a Next Time)...that if your shoes hurt, it doesn't mean there is something wrong with your *feet*. The shoes do not *fit*. Would you be all wounded and depressed if someone told you your nose was purple? No. Because you know it isn't! But a new dose of rejection makes us remember everything negative we have stored about ourselves in that bedrock of childhood rejection. We agree with our rejecter and fail to check our facts with our Creator. Only God and His truth will love the wounded little child within, who got left behind.

He *knows* us. He *loves* us. He *sees* us. Only God can love us enough, will tell us what we need to know:

We do *not* have to be the World's Greatest Anything.

We do *not* have to justify our existence.

We do *not* have to *earn* the right to breathe the air.

We *do* have to choose to trust God's love.

"I cannot *feel* it," we murmur inside. Too many bad examples and crooked friends.

We can't start with *feeling* it. We start with *choosing* it. And that starts with the facts. And those are in the Bible. An "embarrassment of riches," in fact, meant to convince you:

We love Him because He first loved us. 1 John 4:19

We are holy, blameless, chosen by God since before the earth. Ephesians 1:4

I am God's child John 1:12

And it is My desire to lavish My love on you 1 John 3:1

Because I love you with an everlasting love Jeremiah 31:3

For in Jesus, My love for you is revealed John 17:26

I am adopted as His child Ephesians 1:5

I am safe. I John 5:18

People Pleasing

We people-pleasers try so hard, but have you noticed how seldom others are actually pleased? The world crucified the only One who was ever perfect.

The religious people who should have recognized Him did not. His followers believed Him, then doubted Him, then misunderstood His mission. Now, 2000 years later, He is still reviled. The butt of secular jokes on sitcoms, the name that makes the jaded young people roll their eyes.

So we are in good company.

Jesus Himself was rejected. "Despised and rejected of men, a man of sorrows and acquainted with grief." (Isiah 53) His answer? "If the world hates you, you know that it hated me before it hated you." (John 15)

So it is an honor to suffer innocently from rejection, to share in the Lord's own rejection. We *share* this with Him. It does not make the pain of rejection, the suffering, go away. It *redeems* it. Transforms it. Turns lead to gold. A reward that will last *forever*.

I cannot go back and be a beloved baby, nor cure the panic disorder that ate the center out of my life plans, then live my life over again. I cannot make myself insensitive to rejection; Lord knows I've tried. But I *can* yield my life and heart and mind to God, I can choose to make Christ the center of my life rather than Self. I can allow Him to use me as whatever kind of vessel He needs at the time instead of agitating to be Something Else all the time. I can make myself available to Him when He needs me. Not sign up for every "good deeds" program to get credit. Big difference.

I do *not* have to earn His love.

Christians are often confused about this. When we are busy doing things we think are Godly, are we doing it as Christian service? Or thinking our "performance" will win us favor with God? I was confused about it myself. Performance? Or my Mission from God?

So, I asked Him to teach me. And He did. Like most things that seem complex, the answer was actually simple:

If you do something to *give* love, it is a Godly service.

If you do it to *get* love, that is "performance."

REBELLION

Maybe you are not a people pleaser at all. Maybe *your* rejection led you to *rebellion* instead. A ninja flash of anger always cocked and ready. Reject the other guy before he can reject you. Disrespect all authority because everyone in your childhood misused theirs. Maybe nobody in your childhood loved and respected your personhood in a healthy way. So, now, all bets are *off*, baby! It's all about *me*. And look out below!

It's an adolescent's way of discharging anger. An adolescent who wasn't quite stunted in early childhood. Just severely enraged before they could quite achieve adulthood. And, seriously, how many *old* rebels do you ever see? Hardly any successful ones either. There are so many "narcissist survivor groups" online now, it is plain this particular wound lives on. And so many addiction groups, pretty obvious how many of us numb those abusive wounds. Building their own families with other survivors, a mercy of the Lord.

Oddly enough, counselors say rebellion is actually a healthier pathology. The *results* are not good. You alienate other people, make bad choices, lie when the truth would do as well, and tear up your life like a horse pawing at the dirt in the corral all the time. But rebellion is a sign of a strong Will. Once you make *your* choice for God, you're halfway there. Instead of a life of "my rights" and "my way" and getting even, and getting your share, and letting anger and revenge poison your body and mind, you choose to surrender your life to God and His will for you. *And you have just the Will to do it.*

It might be harder to say "no" to your strong-willed flesh that's served you so well, made you a "survivor" instead of a "victim." Strong-willed enough to be capable of standing firm in the Truth, once you know it. Because being a rebel is just another way of being a misfit. But the *reward* is just as huge.

You are special to Him and can choose to trust His will and purpose, listen for his voice.

Or be the cartoon dog Scrappy Do, barking' up a storm for nothing' your whole life. Hiding behind some scary false persona to protect yourself. Putting up walls no sane person would try to breach.

So if you are a rebel...a "punk"...resistant to all authority? Scripture doesn't say God calls you "bad"...just *"unprofitable"* (Hebrews 13:17) He can't *use* somebody like that.

Yet.

Sure there's lots of things in this fallen world it would be better to resist, to rebel against. And God will help you do that, will put that stubborn heart of yours to good use...once you surrender to *His* will instead of hanging with sweaty self-centered hands onto your *own*.

You choose to make your *identity* about God instead of your punk little free-spirited way....you will be put to a higher use than any of us.

The irritant of all our trauma is a grain of sand that is making a pearl. A million little faith steps laid down around wounds. A million mornings to choose His will instead of ours. A million chances to share it with someone and get to see *their* trauma turn into glory. A million hopes for zooming out of all of it eventually and looking back to see it all like shooting stars behind us, knowing we cannot lose it.

That cannot "abandon" us. It is *forever*.

This "Identity" thing is so huge, so eternal, that God even gives us one last related promise, near the end of Revelation:

"To him who overcomes, I will give some of the hidden manna. I will also give him a white stone with a new name written on it, known only to him who receives it." (Revelation 2:17)

Oh, I still remember how I loved that verse when I first saw it years ago. A *new name*! Engraved into a *white stone*! All the things nobody knows but

God, and He preserves and cherishes it *forever.* Nobody to please, nobody to beat down and run away from.

Did looks ever get you that? Or money? Or fame?

See? Only *God* knows who we *really* are. And He sets it in *stone.*

Forget about that "True Self" the psychologists talk about. You become who you *choose* to be; you aren't some hidden shadow locked in a closet somewhere that you have to locate.

Forget singing "I Gotta Be Me" all day, too. It didn't really do it for you, did it? But something will. Something yet to come. A white stone with a new name. Pure. Perfect. New.

A new identity. And no one will remember the old one. The dirty, stained, depressed, drunk, whiny, broken, ugly you, staggering through the wilderness. Nope. You'll be there, you'll be "you." But like He meant for you to be all along. As if the world was not fallen, as if the devil hadn't ravaged your soul. The person you would have been in the Garden. Safe. Loved. Forever.

Motherless Child

Traditional Spiritual

Sometimes I feel like a motherless child

Sometimes I feel like a motherless child

Sometimes I feel like a motherless child

A long way from home

WILDERNESS TIPS

Scripture says it is an *honor* to share in Christ's sufferings,
so why wouldn't it be an honor to share the rejection?
People who do not have a wounded heart will not understand.
Don't expect them to.
You feel different because you *are* different.
God made you special, knows your frame.
People with perfect *flesh* will be a problem for you.
That is why you must walk in the Spirit.
You will never be as pretty, as rich as you *think* you should be.
Go deeper.
Your mother cannot be your Savior.
Your father cannot be your Savior.
Your spouse cannot be your Savior.
Only Jesus is your Savior.
Do it for "eternal weight of glory,"
not the things we leave here.
Do not let them tell you who you are.
Only God knows who you are.

--Patron Saint of Misfits

Judas

I will call *this* "Beloved" Judas, and will tell his story myself because he is gone now. Even the Bible Judas never told his own story.

Our Judas was undeniably the town pervert. And unaccountably a loving father. The tricky thing about the devil is that he's so *persuasive*. Attractive, too.

No wonder Lucifer persuaded a third of the angels in heaven to rebel when he did. Now we are stuck with them, here on this ol' fallen planet. Many of us mad at *God* for the bad things that happen. Nope. He gave us all Free Will. Even the bad guys. Even the fallen angels. We have to live in the "Lucifer Room" down here alright. Lies and temptations everywhere. But once we know the holy goal, it makes all the difference.

Our Judas molested many girls, abandoned a son for being gay, abused his daughter, started his own "church." What to think? When he also seemed to love us?

You *can* still *love* someone that bent. We did. Hated him sometimes too. Yes, he ruined a lot of lives. Those who knew *his* early life of violence and abuse sort of understood. We didn't trust him, or spend time with him. But when we remember him, we know we can't always tell "wounded" from "evil."

Which is why, we know now, the Lord insists we *not judge*. Or seek *revenge*. How can *we* tell a wheat from a weed? How do *we* know the *wounded* from the *evil*?

115

He is gone now. Did he throw away the silver coins and hang himself like the disciple Judas? No. Repent? Not ours to say. We just know it would hurt *us* more than *him* if we hated him now.

THE DEVIL ON YOUR SHOULDER

Who Ya Gonna Believe?

The devil who rules this world has blinded the minds of those who do not believe. II Corinthians 4:4

Our struggle is not against flesh and blood, but against the rulers, against the authorities, against the powers of this dark world and against the spiritual forces of evil in the heavenly realms. Ephesians 6:12

In 2016 a young man by the name of Eric Devin Masters was convicted of tying an 18 month old toddler to a motel bed and raping her while making a videotape to sell to pedophiles.

Here's what the horrified judge said:

"You took an 18-month-old little girl, an innocent little girl, to a motel with the specific intent, with a camera, with straps. You stripped this little girl down, you tied her arms and legs to the bedposts. You proceeded to rape this child. And when you were done, you urinated on this child. I can't imagine a human being doing that. There is just no justification, there is just no excuse for this."

And then he sentenced him to 50-200 years in prison.

In 1991 a little blonde girl was walking from her home to the school bus stop. Jaycee Dugard, then eleven years old, was kidnapped by a sex offender and his wife, and held prisoner for 18 years in their back yard shed. Pregnant at 13, she eventually bore two children by her captor. Alone. Afraid. Depressed. No idea how to get away or where to go. Only a fifth grade education, raising her own babies alone in a shed.

Years ago I even remember a young college man, Mark Kilroy, being kidnapped on the Mexican border while on spring break. They eventually found his body. A satanic gang of drug lords took him to a ranch where he was tortured then murdered in a human sacrifice ritual, his brain removed and boiled in a pot. Their leader had told them that human sacrifice granted them immunity from law enforcement for their drug smuggling operations.

There are many horrific stories like these on the internet. Some things in this old fallen world are so horrible we quit talking about them at all. TV news people mention them, but even *they* quit. Just. Too. Much.

The courts are full. Yet politics and terrorists own the evening news. Everyone's waiting for the world to be engulfed in flames. When it already is.

No mistaking the *evil* in the world.

Pretty plain that there is someone who hates us and wants to steal our souls.

What? Too much?

You might as well know.

Whether you are so sure you have it all that you've quit looking.

Or lost without hope in suffering.

Someone hates you, envies you, and wants to cheat God out of your eternal soul. You hear the whispers? The lies? Embedded so deep you think they are part of *you*.

Some *happy lies* that loving parents pass on: Have nice things! Be good-looking! Ain't this money/house/fame wonderful? Demand respect! It all about *you*!

Some *sad lies* toxic parents and evil abusers pass on, yelling how you are bad or worthless or lying or...things you *never* wanted to be, hope you *aren't*... but your brain stores anyway.

THE DEVIL KNOWS OUR WEAK SPOTS

Especially us wounded ones. He saw our rejections and fears and sadness and wants you to be crushed by them, or pass it on.

Hear his whispers?:

Nobody loves me

Life is not worth it

I'm too ugly

I'm not smart enough

I'm afraid to try...I'll fail

I've already tried everything

I don't deserve any better

I don't have the willpower

The devil and his cohorts talk their trash into our wounded souls over and over.

Until we say "NO!"

And you *gotta* say *no*. Or he will own you. Destroy you, if he can. The devil and his evil minions see those wounds and, if we don't fill them with *God* and *His* Truth, they swarm in and set up camp. Think about the worst offenders you've known or heard of--pedophiles and narcissists and rapists and assassins—what else could have even planted such things in the mind of a human? We do have to decide who to invite into our wounded souls. The sooner the better.

Listen…there is someone who *loves* you and wants you to live with Him forever! Someone who knows all your dirty little secrets, knows what your heart *really* needs. Instead of the empty promises you cling to.

Shhhhh…Listen:

I love you! You are my child forever! Look up, say what I say: You are holy! Beloved! Chosen in Love! Good, not bad! You are safe, you are loved, you are not alone. The tears were a gift, the Bad Thing not for nothing. I will turn it ALL to good!

You don't have to change, try harder, clean up, or anything you don't think you can do to measure up, deserve it, win that love.

Just go to the light.

Or stay in the dark.

Maybe you prefer the darkness…so familiar. But can you deny the hunger, the longing, that teasing hope that there is more to life? The nagging fear you are going to live forever with regret?

The one who hates you tries to keep you in the dark. Without wings. Wounded or puffed up. Crippled in your soul.

The one who loves you tells you the *Truth*…but only if you want to hear it. Our *own* truth was a crazy-maker, that's for sure. But He turns it all to good somehow.

God causes **all** things to work together for good to those who love Him…
(Romans 8:28)

If there was another way we would have found it by now, huh? We've tried everything we could get our hands on to be happy, haven't we? Now we need to try the one we need. The perfect Misfit, the One who knew us all along. Murdered for preaching love and forgiveness!! The world sure wasn't having any of *Him* either.

So we are in good company. Better to believe who *He* says we are than the labels the liar tapes to our backs.

We are *not* what happened to us. *Not* the words the devil whispers, or fallen people say. No. Not mistakes. Not ruined forever. God *loves* us. Knows us. Wants us for *His* family! There's a reason you never trusted *God* before. You thought He was like everybody else. Waiting to tell you what you did wrong. Or worse.

NO!

There's a reason you never looked into the basement of your own soul. Afraid to turn the corner for the smell that wafted up the dark steps down. You didn't want to face what you knew you couldn't *fix*. You knew there was no one to love you, keep you safe, hold your hand, while facing the carnage there. Because there never was!

Until now.

That is the simple beauty and power of the gospel: we find out who we *really* are by discovering who the creator of the universe *says* we are. *Him* we might believe. His love never shames us.

No, we didn't deserve the Bad Thing that happened to us.

Neither do we deserve the grace that transforms it all.

The suffering. The grace. The glory.

That is the holy journey.

Our struggle is not against flesh and blood, but against the rulers, against the authorities, against the powers of this dark world and against the spiritual forces of evil in the heavenly realms. (Ephesians 6:12)

*How great is the love God has lavished on us, that we should be called chil-dren of God! And that is what we are! The reason the world does not know us is that it does not know Him. (*1 John *3:1)*

*We can never be separated from God's love (*Romans 8:39)

*We become God's children (*Galatians 3:26)

STILL LOVIN' THAT DARK SIDE?

The devil makes it look good, draws us in, tries to convince us. Our struggle is not new. It was always that way. The devil even tried it all on Jesus Himself. Chapter four of Matthew tells of Jesus' temptation in the desert:

Then Jesus was led by the Spirit into the wilderness to be tempted by the devil. After fasting forty days and forty nights, he was hungry. The devil came to him and said, "If you are the Son of God, tell these stones to become bread."

Jesus answered, "It is written: 'Man shall not live on bread alone, but on every word that comes from the mouth of God.'"

Then the devil took him to the holy city and had him stand on the highest point of the temple. "If you are the Son of God," he said, "throw yourself down. For it is written:

"'He will command his angels concerning you,

and they will lift you up in their hands,

so that you will not strike your foot against a stone.'"

Jesus answered him, "It is also written: 'Do not put the Lord your God to the test.'"

Again, the devil took him to a very high mountain and showed him all the kingdoms of the world and their splendor. "All this I will give you," he said, "if you will bow down and worship me."

Jesus said to him, "Away from me, Satan! For it is written: 'Worship the Lord your God, and serve him only.'"

Then the devil left him, and angels came and attended him.

See? We aren't the only ones. Evil tried to wreck Jesus' mission from the start too, aiming at His hunger and exhaustion. Just like those evil spirits know what *our* weak spots are too.

With many of us it's *rejection*...and O baby, does he know how to get that one activated! Lots of people out there willing to go along with him, apparently. Hurt us, ignore us, and worse. Sometimes we blame God for those crushing blows. *No.*

Then the devil tried to get Jesus to want *worldly* "kingdoms" instead of *Godly* ones. Kinda like we want stuff or fame or beauty instead of holiness, humility, faithfulness.

The devil even tried to pervert *scripture*...make Jesus fall for the Word wrongly applied.

Maybe that's what our "Judas" did by starting his own church? Had his own version of the Word? Who knows? Just don't kid yourself...the evil spirits can do that too.

WHAT GOD SAYS TO DO ABOUT IT

We just watched a person do this to someone in our family. Took actual scripture verses to falsely accuse them and try to make *himself* look "Christian." Hardly. It was confusing at first, as we all revere God's Word. Even when the perversion of it was plain, we were hard-pressed to know how to fight back. But we did, by faith, begin to answer the perverted verses back with God's own word, *rightly* used. Like Jesus did way back then. Spoke God's Word out loud when our souls suffered the crushing blows.

Doesn't usually work on the other guy. But it sure works for us. Heals our shattered souls. Reminds us who *He* says we are.

So if you have someone who hates you, berates you, controls you, be extra vigilant here. Don't *accept* the pain and shame, for one thing. Then search scripture for the Word *rightly* used. Ask a pastor or trusted Christian counselor to help you if you are still confused. Above all, just do not *fall* for it! Do not berate *yourself* when you can smell the evil intent behind *their* words. The love behind God's Word will show you.

Make yourself a list of Scriptures. Maybe ask someone you know and trust to do it too. Sit in the chair, Bible in hand, and ask the Lord, see where He leads. Or research scriptures online and pray the Lord help you select the best ones. Then read them out loud, write them on cards, tape some to the walls. Whatever it takes to keep God's Word more heavily in the atmosphere than the trash the devil talks.

Yes, it takes time. O yes, very worth it. Life-saving. Soul-saving. Do not eat the fruit the devil hands you anymore. He will always whisper it to us. Just don't fall for it. Adam and Eve did and we all suffer for it still. But Jesus closed the gap and made a bridge we can come to Him anytime we want.

In my own childhood there was ample evidence of evil in the man I called "Judas." Him fondling or even raping female relatives, "playing" with us young girls by wearing an apron with a cloth penis sewn onto it, showing us dirty pictures in another room, taking us across the Mexican border all dressed up to "eat out" and meeting shady characters in dark alleys to exchange items from the trunk.

But he also seemed to care about our wellbeing, our happiness. He was truly devoted to his own daughter. She's the one who told us why he was so perverted. Yes, rooted in his *own* childhood of violence, poverty and abuse. Had to do horrible things to survive on the streets. "Pass it on," the spirits whisper. And many do. *Our choice*!

> Jesus told them another parable: "The kingdom of heaven is like a man who sowed good seed in his field. But while everyone was sleeping, his enemy came and sowed weeds among the wheat, and went away. When the wheat sprouted and formed heads, then the weeds also appeared.
>
> "The owner's servants came to him and said, 'Sir, didn't you sow good seed in your field? Where then did the weeds come from?'
>
> "'**An enemy did this**,' he replied.
>
> "The servants asked him, *'Do you want us to go and pull them up?'*

"*'No,' he answered,* 'because while you are pulling the weeds, you may uproot the wheat with them. Let both grow together until the harvest. At that time I will tell the harvesters: First collect the **weeds and tie them in bundles to be burned**; then gather the wheat and bring it into my barn.' (Matthew 13:24-30)

So it's pretty plain the Lord Himself will take care of it all someday. Ours is not to hate or take revenge. Ours is simply to decide who to believe:

No three philosophers have ever agreed on what perfect truth is, but scripture is plain: It is **"impossible for God to lie"** (Hebrews 6:18), and **Satan is the "father of lies** and the truth is not in him" (John 8:44).

So how, exactly, do we learn to recognize the lies and the Liar behind them? Jesus, the Great Physician, gave the exact prescription:

"If you abide in My Word, then you are truly disciples of Mine; and you shall know the truth, and the truth shall make you free" (John 8:31-32).

Abide in Him (yield yourself to Him body, soul, and spirit, study His Word), and you will know the truth ... about God, about yourself, about others.

Once we know the truth, we *see* the lies and they lose their power. They do not disappear, but they cease to engulf and overpower us. While we were in bondage to the lies, we could only do what *felt* right. Now we can choose what *is* right. Big difference.

Don't get me wrong. It ain't easy. Some of us are...like me..."easy pickins". Not good at fighting back, too vulnerable to negative thoughts, too closed off for fear of rejection. Breakthroughs don't come all at once. We see one, we decide to fight it. Then another comes along. A great verse describes the process:

> *We are destroying speculations and every lofty thing raised up against the knowledge of God, and we are taking every thought captive to the obedience of Christ.* (II Corinthians 10:5)

Like that. You sniff out a negative, hateful, or just plain wrong notion you've had. You find scripture that confirms your suspicion that it just ain't "right." And you choose to think, believe, say, walk in *that* truth instead.

It's not easy. It's a battle. It's worth it.

But not everything comes from the devil. Bad things also come from "the world" and the "flesh." It's just that the devil knows how to take advantage of them.

THE WORLD

> *Do not love the world or anything in the world. If anyone loves the world, love for the Father is not in them. For everything in the world—the lust of the flesh, the lust of the eyes, and the pride of life—comes not from the Father but from the world. The world and its desires pass away, but whoever does the will of God lives forever."* (II John 2:15-17)

Not much to say about the world. We get our ideas about family life from cheesy sitcoms, our introduction to the God-given gift of sexuality from porn, and our yardstick of happiness by what advertisements are selling us. There's worse too: cults, mind control, websites for pedophiles, violent and perverted song lyrics, raunchy secular humanism for lunch, euthanasia for dinner, all pumped out in TV, radio, internet, cell phone apps, tweets, texts. Pounding our eyes and ears and minds 24/7 with everything vile the world has to offer. It's a filthy place.

Or a beautiful place.

Families still gather to pray and trees still ruffle on the horizon. Babies still squeeze your heart, love is still the most powerful force in the universe. God still speaks to hearts that open to Him, same as thousands of years ago.

The "world" is clearly "fallen" from God's original intent. We have to be careful not to believe everything we hear. Try to hold it all up against the yardsticks we find in scripture.

And because many of us were born into an extra "fallen" part of the world, we have to learn to deal with our own scars and misconceptions.

THE FLESH

The "Flesh" is that part of you that wants what it wants when it wants it, consequences or values be damned, even if it's contrary to God's will. Our "default position." We know what it is. We feel its pull every day. Even the apostle Paul suffered from it:

> "I know that nothing good dwells in me, that is, in my flesh;
> for the willing is present in me, but the doing of the good
> is not. For the good that I want, I do not do, but I practice
> the very evil that I do not want." (Romans 7:18-19)

And isn't that just as good a description of our daily struggle as you've ever heard?!

Even if you are "in Christ," sealed by faith and baptism, filled with His Holy Spirit, you know you are not perfect. That something in you wants your own way. *That is your flesh.* It never changes. It has a pattern, developed over your whole lifetime. But it does not have to be your *boss.*

Sometimes you don't do it. Sometimes you do. The flesh is strong. But God is stronger. Ask anybody in AA.

Everything that happens to us in our lives forms our "flesh." The abuses, neglect, rejection of our early childhood forms the wide hidden base, unseen, dangerous. Our God-given instincts are warped. Simple pleasures become addictions. Our freedom becomes indulgence, licentiousness. Our wrong thinking becomes deep ruts in our brain.

But that is not our *spiritual* condition. When we have Christ, the "old man" is gone, regenerated. We are a "new creature in Christ." (I Corinthians 5:17) But a new creature with the same ol' flesh patterns. Rebellious, self-centered, hates to be told what to do, always seeking to satisfy its hungers with anything except God's truth, beauty, goodness. That is the war we fight.

Before Christ we were *enslaved* to this flesh. Didn't know any better; couldn't get free if we *wanted* to. Now we have *freedom* to *choose* a better way. Not perfectly. Not all the time. But some. And then some more.

And we get our lessons in unlikely places. I remember a night many years ago, saying prayers with my ten year old daughter. One of the ornery little girls in her class at school had just had a party...and invited everyone but her. I fumed, cussed, snorted and cried. Wanted something bad to happen to the child who hurt my baby. That night we chatted a minute before prayers. We were planning a slumber party and talked about who she would invite. She named the odious little girl my flesh wanted to slap silly.

"What?" I snorted, unbelieving. "You want to invite *her* to your party?!?! After what she did to you?"

"Well, yes," she answered. Simple, easy. Then she looked in my face. "I wouldn't want *anybody* to feel as bad as she made me feel, mama."

My flesh died an instant blazing death. A brief spark of shame, yes, at my own fleshy reaction from the beginning. Then a holy, peaceful joy that my child could choose that well, that easily, that surely. And that early in her life.

And that is the battle. Every minute of every day.

> *For though we walk in the flesh, we do not war according to the flesh, for the weapons of our warfare are not of the flesh, but divinely powerful for the destruction of fortresses. We are destroying speculations and every lofty thing raised up against the knowledge of God, and we are taking every thought captive to the obedience of Christ, and we are ready to punish all disobedience, whenever your obedience is complete.*
> (II Corinthians 10:3-6)

So that is how the devil traps us in this fallen world. Each of us has fallen "Flesh." He knows how to use both to his own warped advantage. Nobody ever said the devil was dumb. Uses our flesh patterns to steer us away from the spiritual path. Uses the ways of the world to blur the lines in our mind, confuse us, dilute the vision of Truth.

We don't like to think about him much anymore, do we? Nah. It's just "bad guys" and "good guys" now.

GOOD NEWS/BAD NEWS

But once you get real with God, you have to get real with the *devil* at some point too. Once we accept God as our hero, we know who the *villain* really is. I never saw a force that didn't have an *opposite* force.

There is a perversion in this world somewhere of every good and perfect gift God intended. Married sex becomes porn, sacramental wine becomes addiction, the fruit of His earth becomes greasy fries and worse.

People who don't believe in God think the devil is some kind of cultural joke. Horns, pointy tail, red satin body suit. But people who know and believe God soon get a sense that there is a force working *against* Him. Once you begin to know and open up to the God who loves you, the winds shift and you smell the presence of someone who does *not* love you. It is the Big Story, the reason you watch movies, the crux of a good book: Good vs. Evil.

To really love your Hero you need to see the Villain. You need to know just who the hero is saving you from.

Superman's Lex Luthor

Batman's Joker

Luke Skywalker vs. the Emperor of the Death Star

The movies, like the old myths and legends, echo the story God has been trying to tell us for so long. When you learn about the villain who opposes God, who holds fallen mankind hostage, you appreciate the lengths God went to, saving us. What it cost Him to set us free, redeem us.

Everybody wants to be mad at *God* because there is so much horrid stuff in this world; they wonder why He didn't make a better one.

Well, He did.

And men and angels chose another way.

Lucifer and the other rebellious angels were exiled to Earth, forever doomed to wander this lower world, looking for other souls to take with them. Misery does, indeed, love company.

Now I understand perfectly how this all seems very much like a fairytale. Angels and devils have been trivialized by our culture for a long time. But this is what the Bible tells us. So you must keep it on the plate.

Here is an actual conversation I had once with a young woman who was in a very dark place. I know she wouldn't mind if I share it:

Friend: I think I chose the dark side a long time ago. Rebellion. I could hide behind it. I told my therapist, it's like a fist-sized hole of black, empty nothingness...

Me: And you *chose* it?

Friend: Yes. I switched over to the darkness long ago, not sure why. The dark side isn't really the "funnest" path, but it's the one I've been used to my whole life. I really can't recall if I was ever even in the light. I think I probably prefer to stay in the dark side, because I don't want to have to rebuild my whole life and my soul all over again. I *chose* the dark side a long time ago and I didn't even know it. It's some kind of sensation that overcomes you and it becomes a part of you. I prefer the dark side, always have. I want more for me, but I've come to accept that, deep down inside, I do not want to switch paths. How would I? I can't make the darkness go away.

Me: No. Not without a *light*.

See? You already know. God is the light in the darkness. The darkness has a name and many shapes. "Legion," in fact. God is light. Only light will dispel darkness. Without light, dark is powerful. But not as powerful as the light.

Do the math.

Hell is just as real as Heaven. But mostly no one wants to talk about it anymore. Hell and the devil are fodder for jokes. But if we *are* going to live forever, aren't there a whole lot of folks we sincerely hope we do *not* have to live with? Psychos and perverts and bullies galore out there. People in whom lust and greed and avarice dwarf our own. Would you really want to spend eternity with people you are afraid to pass on the streets?

So, then, you ask, why doesn't God just kill all the bad people and leave the good ones?

If you had a *child* who disappointed you, would you kill him? No. Remember Free Will? Love? And there is always the chance for redemption, as long as a person lives. God *never* gives up on us.

Some people listen; some people don't.

This world is ruined, broken. God did not ruin it. He created it perfect. *We* ruined it. God Himself, unwilling to take back the gift of Free Will and turn us into a bunch of puppets, lowered Himself into the muck and showed us the way out. The only way the devil can win now is if we refuse to follow the Lord out.

The devil and his reps know how to *look* good. You know—style over substance. Beauty, fame, power, riches are what he tempts you with. Or easy escapism, if you are really easy to cheat. (What could be easier than watching TV for hours every day? Doing drugs and skipping Life all together?)

If there are lies, there must be a liar, and a perfect truth against which they hurl themselves. If there is truth, there must be a Truth-teller, and a way to find Him. Jesus didn't say he knew *some* truth, or was *like* truth; He said he WAS truth.

So don't dance with the devil. He wants you to be as miserable as he is. And his demons that beset you every day, whispering damaging things in your unguarded ear? Be sorry for them...they missed God's cure through Jesus. They aren't going' to Heaven. But don't *agree* with them, and go along with their suggestions. Don't buy it. Be "wise as serpents, innocent as doves," like God says. (Matthew 10:16)

There are only two "forevers." You can choose yours any time.

"Be alert and of sober mind. Your enemy the devil prowls around like a roaring lion looking for someone to devour."
(1 Peter 5:7-9)

Holy Rain

The devil had his say Lord, but no longer.

Not today.

Rain on me today, Lord, wash me, make me new.

Help me love the other broken people.

Not expect them to be careful of me and my needs.

Help me trust Your love.

Help me do Your Will.

Rain on me, Lord, rain Your will on me.

I lift my face to you, wanting only what You want.

Let Your rain wash the rest of my worldliness and flesh from me.

Let your Love make me what you wanted me to be all along.

Help me to serve You, no matter where you call me.

Or don't call me.

With my weak and wounded will, I accept Your perfect one.

Your holy rain.

--The Patron Saint of Misfits

David

I have lived most of my life in prison. But in an odd way, that's OK. It was "home." I never really knew what "home" was, just lived wherever they took me. Foster homes, children's homes, adoptive homes. I always rode my bicycle or walked away from housing, from school, from everyone. Sometimes made it back to the orchards where I grew up with my sisters and brothers. Eventually always got picked up by the police and returned. Then moved again. Then over again.

While still young, I was sent to Juvenile Detention for petty crimes, then jail for minor crimes. Always just turned myself in, ramped it up a bit. Mostly just hanging with other kids doing or selling drugs or breaking in to stores. Until I hurt a woman. That's what it took. "Home" in prison through all my adult years.

Childhood? I remember loving my baby brother Tommy, giving him his bottle, playing with him. Remember grabbing handfuls of white bread from a loaf on the counter and heading outdoors to play. Our mother always drunk or asleep or yelling.

Once an older boy raped me in our house while other kids watched through the window in the back door, laughing. My drunk mother saw too. Put a scarf on my head and said I must be a girl.

I never knew my father. Just that my mother always said he was in prison somewhere and that I was going to end up just like him. I didn't even know what prison *was* back then. When she got mad at me for anything she yelled at me for being just like him. Then, one day, extra mad, extra drunk, she threw baby Tommy in the back seat of her car and peeled out of the driveway, gravel hitting the side of the house and my legs.

Before long, police came and us kids were riding in their back seat. They drove slowly by a fiery car wreck, smashed into a palm tree at the side of the road. I could see it was mother's car. Could hear the policemen talking about it. I never saw "home" or my sisters or my mother or baby Tommy again.

They put me with families—"foster homes," they called them. Then, every winter when it got cold, they moved me to another one. Then one winter to a "Children's Home" with a lot of kids. By then I was big enough to run away. So they moved me to another "foster home." And the next time it was cold, moved to another.

I got adopted when I was eleven. I didn't even know what that meant. They changed my name to the man's name. Many people gave me gifts and took me places and bought me things. But I never would stay in school. I knew how close it was to "home," so I left and rode my bike there all the time. Best I could find it. Always picked up eventually by the police.

The man—"Dad"—took me to doctors and teachers and church and camping and hunting and fishing. Hoping I would make the son he never had, probably. But I never did. While waiting for him at the golf course I broke into cars and stole radios and stuff. More police, "Dad" lecturing, taking me with him to pay people back. When hunting with him and his friends, I stayed in camp and drove one of the cars around, smashing it into the others. Just never knew what normal was or how to pursue it.

When it got cold I told him "guess I'll be moving soon." He laughed. Then I heard him ask the social worker lady about that when she came. And they both laughed because they could see I did always move when it got cold.

They gave me model car kits to build because I was good at it, kept me busy for hours. They admired them, showed them around. Then, when no one was looking, I set fire to them, watched them melt down into a black lump of twisted plastic. Thought of baby Tommy in the back of the burning car.

Once, after parole, I lived in a tiny trailer and "Dad" lived with me and taught me how to cook and wash my clothes, tried to help me learn how to get a job. But soon I was back at the only kind of work I ever *could* do— stealing, breaking in places, hanging with people who sold drugs. Jail again. Then again. Always walking up to a policeman when I didn't want to live on the streets any more.

One night I saw a lady at the convenience store. She smiled at me, so I followed her home. Waited outside until all was dark and quiet, then broke in. Part of me knew it was wrong, but part of me thought she wanted it. I never meant to hurt her.

Anyway, I learned a lot in my prison "home." I have Bibles from visiting preachers and letters from nice people. And I believe in God now. He keeps me safe. He even brought me a good woman who loved me enough to marry me, live outside the prison, visit when allowed. Many beautiful things I would never have had. It is all I know. It is enough.

Chapter
Eight

OUR SECRET SUPERPOWER

"I Did It Myyyyy Wayyy"

> There are two kinds of people: those who say to God "Thy will be done," and those to whom God says "all right then, have it your way." C.S. Lewis

So now we *know* what happened, the evil that can beset us, lie to us. The "world" that is so ruined. The "flesh" that wants what it wants all the time. Now we see what we need to fight.

But how? It's hard and it's uphill. How to come to believe what God says about us (holy, beloved, chosen) instead of our lifelong default flesh patterns (bad, unloved, nobody cares)? How to fight off those ugly evil whisperings that never go away and choose God's Truth instead? Actually make new *pathways* in our broken brains?! Medical studies say it is possible. But they aren't saying it's easy. So many never do. So many miss so much because they give up the fight.

My adoptive brother, "David" had only neglect, perversion, and violence in his childhood. He was eleven years old when the Welfare Department asked my folks to take him, after three years in various foster homes. I was about to leave for college, but spent some time with him before I did. The stories he told me were things a kid this age couldn't make up. And so horrid that even I couldn't make myself share them. As if it was my secret to keep too.

Years later, I went with our adoptive father to the hospital to talk to the woman he had threatened to rape. She was a kind woman who forgave everything once she heard his story. We could all just tell he had no way to know what "normal" was in his entire life. We tried to help him change when we adopted him, but by then, when he was eleven, it was too late.

I remember clearly the many model cars he built and torched. Remember how kind and smart and charming and lost he was. I loved him, but knew he couldn't live in the real world.

He has spent most of his adult life in prison. Where else would a child with a script like that end up? A sweet soul, good mind, people skills were all his. But his damaged early childhood derailed him all the time. He never *chose*, only followed, until, like water, he fell to the lower levels.

It took *prison* to hold him still long enough to *see*. But he finally did. Then he *chose*. And the Lord brought His own mercies into that dark place and built a life for him.

No, not the life we wished he would have. But a life that keeps him safe.

There are thousands of stories from the horror of the Nazi concentration camps that illustrate this. One famous survivor sums it up:

> *"We who lived in concentration camps can remember the men who walked through the huts comforting others, giving away their last piece of bread. They may have been few in number, but they offer sufficient proof that everything can be taken from a man but one thing: the last of the human freedoms -- to choose one's attitude in any given set of circumstances, to choose one's own way."* Viktor Frankl, "Man's Search for Meaning"

This is the only kind of "free" you can be in prison. Or in suffering. We can choose what to *think*. To think like God says. Or the world. Or the flesh. We can *choose* that wherever we are.

FREE WILL—GOD'S GIFT TO US *AND* THE BAD GUYS

The devil does *not*. His way is to *trap* vulnerable people. Ensnare them. And *not* offer them any "free will" to get out. Drugs, sex, gambling, gluttony, hoarding, crime, abuse...a million traps. None with the freedom to *choose* once you are ensnared.

We recently watched a lovely young Christian woman emotionally abused by a very controlling narcissistic man. She had no idea when she married him, but quickly got the picture. Not safe to have a different opinion, constantly accused of bad motives, forced to slip around quietly to try to keep the peace. Nothing left in "their" house for *her*.

Except her *thoughts*, her *faith*. And we watched it save her. Gave her strength and wisdom to let the Lord Himself unfurl the ugly truth then *set her free*. Kept her from losing her own way as it played out, as thousands of victims do. Will no doubt minister that gift to other victims in her life.

Easier on us if we use it *before* we are trapped. But not always possible. The devil, as we have seen, is very clever and attractive.

But still there for us *after*. A longer, harder road. But the same gift awaits.

In prison, or addiction, or beset in any way, God infuses our choice for Him with a power no other choice in life ever offers. A *superpower*. Truly. The only one that tops *all* of them.

If we choose it. If we use it.

Some of us wounded ones have "I can't" as our default position. God wants us to see we *can*...that His grace is always available to help us resist the negative whisperings. We put Him on those wounds in our soul, God Himself will turn them to good.

As a child, we all played "superhero" and thought about our "superpowers." I couldn't decide between *invisibility* and *flying* for mine. Both had their charms; both had capes and costumes and amazing vehicles. I could slip around unseen or fly away at will. Either, in my mind, would be better than strength or telling the future or x-ray vision or anything I could think of.

Little did I know then what my secret super power *really* was. It wouldn't have taken me so long if a comic book superhero had talked about it. Or if there was a cape or costume for it. *Free Will is the sword in the stone!* With new discoveries in neuroscience we are beginning to see how our *thoughts* can change the actual neurons of our brains.

And the gift is already ours. Maybe damaged, dinged, or weakened by the kryptonite in our childhoods and environments, our weak flesh. But there. Inviolable. A gift from God. We can't always control what *happens* to us, but we can choose how we *think* about it. We can. I wished I had a cape of invisibility. I dreamed I could fly. But now I try to base my life on *reality*, not wishes and dreams.

Once I paid a clinic $300 to do "Aversion Therapy"...trying to lose weight. Chocolate was my main addiction, so they sat me in front of a huge mirror and had me eat chocolate while they wafted a vial of scent that smelled like poop under my nose. Gave me negative messages about the gross smell, the ugly brown on my teeth. Do you think it made me hate chocolate? No it did not. From then on, every time I smelled *poop*, I wanted chocolate.

And that's about the luck I had with worldly "power."

No, the only *real* power I found in my life was this one. The gift God *gives* but we don't always *use*.

BLACK DOG, WHITE DOG

The one you feed more will do better.

Most people are aware there are two opposite forces at work inside their own soul. Various people over many years have called this the "White Dog" and the "Black Dog." And the one who *wins* is the one we *feed* the most.

White Dog: As a Christian, there is a part of us that is like Jesus: loving, compassionate, honest, and focused on helping others. We pray and choose to live by His higher standards, not our low ones. Want to walk "in the Spirit."

Black Dog: The other part is our "Flesh." By default self-centered, whiny, sullen, angry, thinking of ourselves, our needs, more than others. We don't always think to *choose God's higher way.*

I asked an agnostic friend once if God could do *one* thing for him, to convince him God was there and loved him, what would it be. Tears filled his eyes. "Get my son off drugs." I told him we would all pray for that. Within months the son was off drugs and in church with his family. A miracle to see, truly.

But not enough to win his father over.

We see what we *want* to see. Choose what we *want* to believe.

God *knows* you, even if *you* don't know *Him.* You're His child and He created you with high hopes for a loving relationship with Him forever. And He gave us each free will. Like the angels. Why? Heck, I don't know.... why do *we* have children? Didn't we know how much trouble they would be? That they would disobey us, rebel? Yet wouldn't we give our very lives for them? Like that.

Love has its reasons.

Three crosses were on the Hill that day. Jesus in the middle, convicted thieves on either side. One of them chose to believe Him and one did not. To the one who believed, He promised paradise that very day.

Jesus made a special point of His own surrender, His own free will choice to follow God the Father's command. *To lay down His very life*. He didn't have to. When He prayed beforehand, in the Garden of Gethsemane, He asked that He not have to. "If it be Thy will, let this cup of poison pass," He begged.

Like we do. Please, please, please. Begging, crying, sweating drops of blood even.

Then He got up anyway, and did the Father's perfect will.

Like we can.

> *No one takes it from me, but I lay it down of my own accord. I have authority to lay it down and authority to take it up again. This command I received from my Father.* (John 10:18)

And that is the journey, isn't it?

First, we *learn* God's will.

Then we *surrender* to it.

Then we *choose* to walk in it.

Or not.

All the time. Every day. Every minute, when the road gets hard.

He Himself teaches you the rest of what you need to know. And He teaches like a good Montessori teacher....a guide. He prepares our environment and guides us into what we are ready to receive.

But He will not do it against our will.

Apart from outright miracles—suspending all the laws of physics and reason—the main way God provides to build our souls in this life is the power to choose our *thoughts*. Power to dismantle all the "me first, that's awful, oh no" kind of toxic thoughts, implant all the "Your will, not mine, thank You Jesus" kind of thoughts.

A powerful two-edged sword we claim when we pull it from the stone of *self*-will.

When you choose the Lord's way, your flesh begins to come under submission to the Holy Spirit within you. That is how we can have the "fruit of the Spirit"—love, joy, peace, patience....Instead of the anger, bitterness, and selfishness we had before.

But that ratty old flesh never dies. It is always with us. The only way to overcome it is this superpower. While we are praying and begging God to *do* something, *fix* something, He is waiting for us to *choose* something.

Some believers have pretty healthy processes and can just decide. And some of us have *very* strong, wounded flesh, resistant to change. The traumas of childhood make us wary, stubborn, numb, or misinformed. It is harder for us. But not impossible. But G*od will never usurp his gift of free will.*

He just will not *make* you do anything, think anything, choose anything.

But if you aim your will towards Him, He will see to it that it meets the mark. This is how nasty old dirty ore mined from the bowels of the earth become pure gold. This is the "refiner's fire." Step, step, choose, choose. "Your will, Lord, not mine." Surrender all to the *holy* journey or stay in the whiny rut of self-centered flesh. Choose it, over and over.

You do not have to choose a church, know any doctrine, or read the whole Bible to get that far. Although any of those things might speed your journey. Sadly, they could slow it down as well. Because evil, always looking to sabotage faith, can make sure you see broken people in boring churches or read bizarre symbolic scriptures. And you have no protection yet. But if you *choose* Him, *ask* Him, He will lead you safely through. The next open door, a new person in your life, a sudden change in circumstances. Until you are no longer surprised by His guidance. Just humbled by His mercy.

And if you don't choose? If you don't ever ask? If you choose and ask and listen and then say "no, I like my way better?"

He leaves you like you were. With a veil over your eyes of understanding. Like a goldfish in a bowl, waiting for the next flakes of food without knowing the real world all around you.

That is what "conversion" really means. Turning from one thing to another. From Self to God. That is what we are doing here, us pilgrims. That is what it is all about. The "Exchanged Life." The "Victorious" Christian life. Born again. A new creature. All the catch phrases you hear and are not quite sure about. You trade your little life and its goals and plans for His.

Now, I don't know about you, but when I was young and sparky, I was perfectly content with my silly little plans for happiness every day. If it felt good, pretty much, I did it. Only when it didn't work for me did I think to look up. I am wilier now. The devil still spends a fair amount of time telling me lies, my flesh still wants what it wants. But I am better at recognizing a dead end now. And better at loving my Savior. Not perfect. But on the best journey of my life.

"He who loses his life will find it," the Good Book says.

SOME PEOPLE LIKE IT. AND SOME PEOPLE DON'T.

The wounds from early childhood made us very susceptible to the lies of the world and whispering spirits from...somewhere else, shall we say. I found it *very* difficult to choose higher, holier thoughts when engulfed in depression and anxiety and health problems.

I mean, it's *hard* to get the part that is the most *broken* to do the work that is most *important*.

At first, it was only tiny little mewling cries of memorized verses ("I have been crucified with Christ"--Galatians 2:20). Or longings ("He will never forsake me"--Hebrews 13:5 and many others). Or days of tears without the energy to speak at all.

Over time it became a braver choice. More insistent. ("Put on the full armor of God"—Ephesians 6:10-17) and more efficient ("Tear down strongholds"—II Corinthians 10:4) as I began to see His way was better.

Then, over the years, an altogether stronger warrior. Never able to "fight" before, now able to confront the one who did not want God's best for me. I learned to talk back:

Bark away, ornery flesh. You are not my boss any more.

God is bigger than you, lousy genes.

Nibble at my edges every day, you jealous demons. I will press forward in spite of you.

Nothing you do can take away my soul, my eternal Spirit. Rob my peace, sometimes even ruin my testimony, but fold when you see the inevitable glory that awaits me. I feel sorry for you, lying demons, but I cannot help you. You are lost. I am saved. Bound for heaven.

That is the only thing that broke the strong-willed horse within. Tamed it. Guided it instead of being carried away by it. Never perfectly. But more and more.

So, if we really want to change—or really want to change the world!—then we have to change our *thinking*. Find the old worn ruts in our brain that parrot the devil's lies, and plant scripture there instead. And science is discovering more and more today, that even gets right down into your physical brain and fixes things you thought were irreparably broken.

I call that a miracle.

Scripture says we "have the mind of Christ." Some of us feel like it might be more like the brain of Frankenstein. But God has His ways. There will be no IQ in Heaven. Only what we did with that free gift. And when we die, our *brain* will die and go back to dust, with the rest of our body. But *not our mind*. Our *mind* is part of our eternal *soul*. We will have it forever. It's a delicate business, learning the difference between your flesh "brain" and your soul "mind," but it can be done.

I had to meditate on it myself, for a long time, to save my own life. Because my flesh *brain* has some glitches in it. I had to learn to choose, with my free will, a million times, to believe what God says about me instead of what my bent flesh brain, family and friends, even doctors, said about me.

You have no doubt seen people in "ministry" that were pure flesh, seeking praise or money or self-satisfaction. On the other hand, you have seen humble services performed by a Spirit-filled person in perfect submission and humility. Even "good works" can be *dead* works, of no profit to the kingdom of God. Depends on which way you *choose*—the Spirit or the flesh.

I had a dear friend who had a lifelong "flesh pattern" of anger. She said it "worked for her" over the years; got results. Kickin' ass and takin' names. Most folks comply just to get rid of you. But for love of God's word, and her own son, she *chose* to give it up. It was a battle over every thought, every idea, every pattern she ever had for getting by in life.

But she kept choosing it, studying God's way and choosing it, over and over. And she, unknown to anyone but a couple of her friends and God, saved her son's life. This was the "call" on her life, her "Mission from God." She chose to say "yes" to God instead of "I did it my way." No one in this world rewarded her, but she is there now with an eternal reward. (We miss you, KP.)

BE WARNED! THERE IS NO PRESTO CHANGE-O

No magic tricks. No instant miracle that makes us perfect.

We can't be a heathen one day and the next a perfect saint. We still need to learn to *use* our superpower. Even Superman needed training. Choices for faith, or for doubt. For obedience, or for rebellion. For love, or for hate. The walk to glory is a million choices between the Spirit and the flesh.

We have to take our mind *back* from the devil. We are grownups now, human beings with an eternal soul. NOT politically correct lemmings repeating the drivel we see on social media or hear in the street.

This is where reading the Bible helps. We have a grad student's impulse to skip the primary source, and go to the secondary ones, read books *about* the Bible, or hear sermons that *explain* the Bible. The devil never ceases his suggestions. But if you can read, and you want the strong ammo, read it yourself. Or listen to it in audio form. Not so we "know stuff" to beat others over the head with. Or to be acknowledged authorities. We do it to learn what God *sounds* like, so we can reject the devil's whispered lies.

For example: You find yourself thinking "I am a loser, I can't do anything right." You laugh at the devil's tired old line and answer back with God's Truth: "I can do all things through Christ who strengthens me!" (Philippians 4:13) and "I am more than a conqueror...." (Romans 8:27).

Mine is always "I'm so scared, maybe I'm dying." God gives me Psalm 118 "I shall *not* die, but *live* and proclaim the works of the Lord."

Like that.

To this day, my own not-Jesus thoughts are Kryptonite. The longer they stay, the weaker I am to fight them. But I keep choosing. I choose to believe God that He conquered Death and my Beloveds are safe in Him forever. Choose to see rejection as an honor I share with him instead of something that will kill me. I still wish there was an easier way. I whine. I complain. Do it wrong, fall back in fits of anger. *Perform* instead of say "no."

But I get to see the miracle again and again when I do it His way instead of mine.

Changing Our Minds

We decide to change our minds;
Not humor it any more,
Or spoil it, or follow it,
But take it firmly in hand
By an act of will.
Some thoughts are dark and tenacious as Fear,
And can only be dragged, bloody,
Back through the original wound.
Hard work.
Like wrestling an alligator.
Or an angel.
Lame, either way,
But blessed.

THE GREATEST EXPRESSION
OF LOVE
IS TO
CHOOSE IT
WHEN YOU DON'T
FEEL IT

Sophie

Mother met men at the front door and they handed her a bottle of booze and she would leave the house. They would come in and talk to me, then put me up on the table in the kitchen and do stuff to me down there. They told me to never tell anybody or they would hurt us.

I never really liked mother. Other kids seemed to like their mothers, so I never said anything. But I was always alone on my birthday, and one time I was playing with my puppy on the balcony and it wiggled between the bars and dropped two stories down and died.

But sometimes my grandma would come get me and I loved her. She cooked for me and no men came to her house. But mother always came again and took me away.

I lived with some other people a while too. It was fun. But then they moved me to someone else's house. I quit thinking anybody loved me enough to let me stay.

When I was 14 I kept a mayonnaise jar full of vodka under my bed. The cure. The numb. The blank years to come. So much more suffering, but who to tell? Who would care? No. Better to just be numb.

The only thing that changed me was getting baptized. Now I know God and love Him and He takes cares of me in spite of everything. Same problems, but I give love to others best I can, my family and at work. And just trust God to work the rest out. Simple. Never look back, just walk through the days. *He* knows. I don't have to.

The Physics of Faith

For Your Inner Agnostic

*Reason's last step is the recognition that there are an
infinite number of things which are beyond it.*
–Pascal

Research is what I'm doing when I don't know what I'm doing.
–Werner von Braun, space engineer

Some things are true whether you believe in them or not.
–*City of Angels* movie

Quarks, black holes, leptons, O my.

We've never seen them. But we "know" they are there.

We take it on faith.

Faith in the physicists and instruments who tell us about them.

Our relationship with God requires some faith too. Partly a gift from Him, partly a choice we make, partly the same kind of agreement we have with physicists and other scientists. We can't study *everything* ourselves, keep physical evidence before us *all* the time. We can't! But for those of us who are misfits, faith is where the healing journey must begin. And very often it has been beaten out of us from the start.

Lots of folks are trying to beat it out of us now. There are sad videos all over the internet and celebrities on TV ranting that "religion" is stupid. *Very* sure there is no God. And with even less evidence than believers have that there *is*.

Years ago, as a young Registered Nurse, I lost my first patient to death. It was my first *physical* experience of something I had heard about all my life: death. I thought I knew about it. I went to the patient's bedside and helped an aide prepare the body. Then the Funeral Home people came into the room with a stainless steel cart and pulled it up alongside the bed. I stood at the head, holding his shoulders, the other nurse stood at the feet. We counted "one, two, three" and lifted to swing the body over to that cart.

Then I was stunned and sickened by a loud metallic crash as the man's head, which I had not thought to support, hit that stainless steel cart, BAM. We were all struck dumb for a moment. Then the funeral home attendants stepped in and covered the body with their heavy vinyl drape emblazoned with the Funeral Home name. Very discreet, nobody would know for sure. And they wheeled him out.

It took me another moment to recover. The phrase I had heard my whole life—"dead weight"—came to mind. And I realized the *idea* of "dead" was nothing like the *experience* of "dead." I would have held his head if I had.

We cannot really "know" anything except by faith. I "knew" that patient was dead by faith in medical findings. But when that skull hit the metal two feet below it, I "knew" in a whole new way.

A lot of people learn about God the hard way just like that. Willfully ignoring the spiritual evidence to make sweeping statements based on nothing but their own rap.

Until they need Him. Or meet Him.

I recently sat with an elderly friend at the hospital who had just met the Lord after a lifetime of denying Him. He had a stroke and told how he felt himself go up. There were some gates, he said. But he didn't think he could go in. But someone told him "Yes, you can come in...you just need to go back and be a little kinder."

My own spirit smiled within me, because he was one of the crustiest, orneriest people I knew. And *was* now sweeter and kinder! He did not have to explain his own transformation.

GOD GIVES US WHATEVER EVIDENCE IT *TAKES*

If we only listen. Say "yes."
Nowhere does God say, in His long story, that faith in Him must be blind. Or even perfect. More like a journey, one willing step at a time, changing, growing, refining all the time. Not unlike science. Scientists take available evidence, compile it into logical theories, propose their theories to other scientists, who refine them with evidence and theories of their own.

Not that long ago, scientists assured us that faith was being replaced by reason, that "creationism" was dead. Today, advanced discoveries in physics have provided some very surprising plot twists that favor *faith*. The "Big Bang," as it is popularly called, is corroborated repeatedly in the lab: Time had a specific beginning. And the *cause* of the universe we can observe must have been *outside* of it when it was created. Just like scripture says.

Physicists' experiments this century have demonstrated the odd characteristics of *light*. Up until now, it was thought to be a particle. Then a wave. The famous "double-slit experiment" proved it exhibits qualities of both a particle and a wave. Yet light still toys with them, seems to change its "mind," almost like a being in its own right. And we wonder. "God is light," scripture says. If we imagine angels the way they are described in scripture, maybe they are too. That would explain a lot.

Many of the stars you see in the sky are actually dead and their long-gone light is just now reaching us here. And there are millions there that we cannot yet see. Who knows what glory remains from the brief blaze of our own lives? Or what "immortality" or "eternity" really mean? Faith studies, theorizes, gathers evidence where it can. Like scientists.

Quantum physics goes on to say that a particle doesn't *exist* in a particular location in space and time until it is *observed*. A 2007 experiment even shows that what happens to a particle in the present can affect it in the past. Impossible, against all reason! Yet true.

Our minds can barely hold on to observable, provable, concrete truths. How could they absorb eternal, omniscient, transcendent Truth?

Only by faith. Faith in the postulations of scientists you will never know, past, present, future, if you want to be a scientist.

And faith in the observations and experiences of ancients who saw God die on a cross and come back to life in three days. So sure of it they were willing to die for their belief. Faith in the record of scripture, which surpasses the bibliographic authenticity of any book in the world. And the faith of millions of believers who have had their lives transformed across the millennia.

My first visit to an observatory illustrated it well. The huge telescopes were set up to find and observe a particular star. The attendant assured me it was set correctly and the star would appear. I saw nothing.

"Be patient," he smiled at me. "Wait. Watch."

Then, miraculously, it appeared out of nowhere, right where the massive telescope was fixed all along.

You have to want to know. You have to have information gathered and proven by others. You have to have faith in the person showing you, in the equipment, in the experiences of others. And wait with patient expectation. Whether for the physics of the universe. Or for the physics of our faith.

164

One of my Beloveds meditates on a certain star as her focal point every night. Sometimes it isn't in the place she estimates. But she knows, now, that if she keeps staring at that spot it will appear in a while. Pop up in the dark vastness and pulse as if to tease "I was here all along."

Faith. The "confidence in what we hope for and assurance about what we do not see." (Hebrews 11:1)

Like scientists, we learn what we can from others, from scripture passed down for thousands of years.

BUT WHAT *IS* FAITH? AND HOW DOES ONE *GET* IT?

Same way the physicists get their faith in what is out there in space: gather information, examine evidence, and choose to accept it, go forward from there.

Scripture says faith comes from what is heard, and what is heard comes through the message about Christ. *Then* we choose to accept it and go forward from there (Romans 10:17).

In rare stunning moments we see how faith heals in spite of everything. The murdered child's mother visits the killer in prison; they weep together. The pope, shot and nearly killed, visits his shooter in prison as soon as he gets out of the hospital, prays with him. The innocent, sinless son of God is brutally beaten and nailed—with iron stakes—to a wooden beam. Writhing in agony, He says "Father, forgive them."

Faith does miracles. Redeems things. Makes them holy.

Did you ever get a postcard from a friend in a beautiful foreign land? "Wish you were here." You look deep into the picture, try to imagine the place. You think of your friend. Maybe even wonder if you might go there someday, see it for yourself. When your friend comes home and tells you more and more about the place, your appetite to see it increases.

That is not unlike the planting and nurturing of faith. Scientist share their findings, believers share their testimonies and experiences.

In general dictionary terms, "faith" is simply "confidence or trust in a person or thing, trust in another's ability." We trust a car to get us somewhere. Or trust a person, maybe our mother, to love us. In gospel terms, "faith" is when we trust Jesus to do and be just what He *said* He was. He said He was the Son of God, sent to enable us to be children of God again.

We *hear* about it, mainly through the Bible, or people telling us about the Bible. And we agree to trust *that* instead of a whole lot of *other* stuff we've heard. Mainly to trust that instead of our *own* power. Like your friend's postcard, you accept it on faith until you have more evidence. And every step of faith makes your relationship with God more real. Brings you more evidence.

It is important to realize that nowhere does any dictionary or any Bible say faith is a *feeling*. You may or may not have any kind of warm, fuzzy feeling associated with faith. Along with our souls, our "feelings" were wounded. They lie to us all the time. They change all the time. We simply cannot *trust* our feelings. It isn't the *feeling* you have when you pray that matters, but the *faith* you have in God's truth.

Over two thousand years ago, Jesus prayed to Father God: "I praise You, Father, Lord of heaven and earth that You have hidden these things from the wise and intelligent and have revealed them to babes." (Matthew 11:25) There is a special innocence and simplicity in the gospel, even while the world grows more jaded and complex. You can know God with faculties that are *higher* than your intellect. Know Him the way mystics always have.

We trust and use dozens of manmade contraptions every day that we do not understand at all. Yet we trust them. It makes perfect sense that God's ways are on a much higher, unfathomable, but trustworthy place. I have confidence the lights will come on when I flip the switch. And a growing confidence God will meet my ever-changing needs. Faith.

ALL YOU CAN BRING IS LOVE

I remember one faith gift for my own little family. One night we were all asleep and my youngest daughter's stereo suddenly came on, blaring much louder than it had ever been played in regular use. My young daughter and I met, startled, running to turn it off, embracing each other in comfort. I soothed her and put her back to bed. In less than a minute the phone rang. My daughter ran to my bedside as I talked. I hung up.

"It's Mimi, isn't it?" she said, her little girl heart sure, eyes big.

"Yes, baby. She just passed away." Her great-grandmother, her namesake, had left this world. And God allowed her spirit to say goodbye to the child she adored on her way to Forever.

Another time I begged the Lord to let me hear from my best friend, who had recently died. And He did. Early one morning, her unmistakable voice and personality were present to me, as if by a great effort. I knew it was her. *"All you can bring is love,"* she told me in her intense whisper. And my heart knew... "Yes." It made perfect sense to me then, makes perfect sense to me now.

I had always thought people mostly made these kinds of things up. Not out of any bad motive, but out of emotional need or something. But when it happens to *you*, you know. God is there and He is not silent. You reach out in faith, He answers in love. He knows your heart, knows your need. It is not *information* He offers, but something deeper. Eternal.

There is an organization that is maintaining a digital archive across time of all internet pages. They call it the "Way Back Machine." Every version of every word and graphic that was ever on the internet can be searched as it was, no matter how many revisions it has gone through. So now it is not enough to know everything. You can know every version of the things every person ever put on the internet. Imagine.

That is why you hear scientists talk about computer power growing so exponentially that they will soon be able to solve problems, develop new information and strategies, faster and better than human intelligence. "Artificial Intelligence," they call it. So you can forget any notion you ever had about how much you can learn or know. You can never learn or know *everything*.

Yet you can put *all* of that "knowledge" *inside* a tiny corner of the universe that was created, "*ex nihilo*," by Someone. God, we call Him. The intelligence that He brings to bear on His creation is something *else*. Something *larger*, deeper, than human *or* artificial intelligence.

KNOWING THE KNOWER

That is the Truth that faith taps in to. That is what we can actually know about "everything." We can know the Knower. Use our finite intelligence to communicate with the infinite intelligence that created it. Scripture is clear that "all things in heaven and on earth, visible and invisible, whether thrones or powers or rulers or authorities; *all things* have been created through Him and for Him." (Colossians 1:16)

Because no matter how many facts you learn, how much you know, how smart you are, your stored knowledge can be destroyed by one car wreck or gunshot to the brain, or Alzheimer's. Anything can happen to that kind of knowledge. The *spirit's* way of knowing is *immortal*.

I figure I already know too much stuff. Some of it haunts me and I wish I could *UN*-learn it. Some of it makes me afraid. For myself, for the world. But when I try to "know" God it is different. Better. Peaceful. Exciting. Always worth knowing.

We had a close family friend who spent seven years in a profound diabetic coma, unable to communicate in any way. Her body permanently curled in a fetal position, eyes wandering without focusing or turning to any voices, she was kept alive by tube feedings. When her eldest daughter died, someone told her, even though we had no expectation she could comprehend. Her eyes could not even make contact with ours. But after they told her, tears slipped silently from the corners of her eyes.

She "knew." And that love for her daughter was safe, held inviolable by her soul. And her soul held inviolable by her Spirit, which, coma or no, was in communion with God. Because she and her family were people of faith. They are all safe together now. She knows everything now. And during those seven years of coma she "knew" all she needed to know as well.

The Bible says that "without faith it is impossible to please God" (Heb. 11:6). It is what He wants. A relationship with us, His children.

It also says the Holy Spirit will then "guide you into all Truth." (John 16:13)

It is hard to understand how all those scrolls and words could have survived thousands of years, if the Creator of the universe did not protect them. Impossible to imagine how else the hundreds of prophecies from hundreds of years prior, could have been so dead-on. Five hundred years *before* Jesus was born, for just one example, Isaiah prophesied that the Messiah, when he died "on a tree" would *not* have his legs broken. And Jesus, on that cross, did not, even though every other crucified victim did. Things like that. Hundreds of them. Our faith, once quickened, does not have to be blind.

GO TO THE LIGHT

Did you ever go into a dark place from a well-lit room? Your pupils will only let so much light in at a time. What seems pitch black at first will slowly, gradually reveal enough light to make out shapes. And we cannot make that happen any faster, no matter what we do. Have faith that God will reveal more and more of His Truth to you, just as you have faith your eyes will adjust and eventually and be able to see, even in a very dim place.

Our journeys are never exactly like anyone else's journey, which I call "good news" indeed. He wants to tell you the story meant for *only you*. A pastor I knew one time had a small sign on his desk: "For God so loved the world that He did not send a committee." Yes.

This Truth is mind-boggling, hard to wrap your mind around. But that doesn't make it less likely, it makes it *more* likely. *Lack* of faith is partly a failure of imagination, not an *excess* like people say. We think too small, not too vast. It is hard to imagine angels. But it is also hard to imagine Black Holes. It is hard to imagine a "devil." But it is also hard to imagine the billions spent on porn every year.

Think about angels for a moment. Beings of light. Spiritual beings with no bodies, no mass, immortal. Only detectable through what they do, how they act on something else. Seem like fantasy? Now think about photons. Likewise, no mass, undetectable except by their action. And, apparently, also immortal, as long as they travel at the speed of light. We can barely begin to comprehend these things, yet they are the fabric of the entire universe.

How can we understand electricity? Or television? Or love? The hydrogen atom (which we cannot see) is held together by the magnetic forces of particles we cannot see.

Do you believe in love? Have you ever done something because of it? You cannot *see* love. Is it so horribly problematic for you that you cannot *see* God? The most powerful forces that control our lives are invisible: electricity, radiation, love and hate.

It is God's mercy that prevents us from seeing Him in this life. Like He told Moses: "you cannot see my face, for no one may see me and live." It would blow all the circuits of our finite little brains, no doubt. As if a massive three-story computer tried to funnel all its information into one tiny chip.

We cannot even actually see light. Just its reflection off of objects and into our retinas. Similarly, everything we need to know about God is reflected in Jesus. "We must walk by faith and not by sight," the Bible tells us. (II Corinthians 5:7).

And there is more and more *evidence* all the time. Science and religion were never the opposite forces people think they are. A long list of reputable physicists concur:

> John O'Keefe (astronomer at NASA): "We are, by astronomical standards, a pampered, cosseted, cherished group of creatures... If the universe had not been made with the most exacting precision we could never have come into existence. It is my view that these circumstances indicate the universe was created for man to live in."

> Arthur Eddington (astrophysicist): "The idea of a universal mind or *Logos* would be, I think, a fairly plausible inference from the present state of scientific theory."

> Vera Kistiakowsky (MIT physicist): "The exquisite order displayed by our scientific understanding of the physical world calls for the divine."

Frank Tipler, Tulane University physicist, believes that
physics has actually proven the existence of God as aligned
with Christian doctrine specifically. He writes that quantum
theory is proven by experimental evidence and that some
physicists deny it because the universe that it describes
begins and ends with God.

In 1927 physicist and astronomer Georges Lemaitre first proposed the
theory that the universe is expanding. Already-renowned Albert Einstein
refused to accept the idea. In 1931, Lemaitre refined his theory of an
expanding universe to include an initial point—what he called the "Primeval
Atom" and, later, the "Cosmic Egg" which exploded at the moment of creation. This theory became known, and was later validated and accepted,
as the "Big Bang," the gold standard of physics today. What you may not
know is that Georges Lemaitre was also a Catholic priest. He gave that paper
describing this seminal work at a conference on how spirituality and the
physical universe relate.

Einstein and other physicists remained skeptical until the 1960's, when
it was proven by the discovery of cosmic microwave background radiation.
The universe is, indeed, expanding, and can be shown to have been created
at a specific point in time. Just as described in Genesis.

In 1933, Lemaitre and Einstein were in California for a conference of
seminars. After the Belgian priest outlined his theory of the origin of the
universe--what would evolve into what is now called the "Big Bang." Einstein
stood and applauded. He is quoted as saying: "This is the most beautiful and
satisfactory explanation of creation to which I have ever listened."

The only thing as big as "The Big Bang" in physics today is "Quantum
Mechanics." Max Plank is considered the founder of Quantum mechanics.
A lifelong Christian, he was an elder in his church from 1920 to his death.

In 1937 he delivered a lecture, "Religion and Natural Science", declaring that both religion and science require a belief in God.

But we live in a very secular age. So many of us have been raised with no faith. Or have walked away from the faith of our families. We have been immersed in the cynicism of the media for more than one whole generation now. And are so overwhelmed with "information" that we have lost the ability to mine for treasures; too busy scanning, scanning, scanning everything superficially.

But we remember the faith, overhear the jargon, eavesdrop on the debates, and our curiosity persists. We have lived long enough to see Science fall from grace, just like Faith did. They taught us as children that the solar system was set in stone, all mapped out and "scientific fact." Then, a few years ago, they decided that no, Pluto was not really a planet.

Science is no *substitute* for God.

God is not expecting us to find Him without evidence. It was never Faith OR Reason. Faith without Reason is more like superstition. Reason without Faith is the dead materialism of our age. For Truth you will use *both*. As Einstein is quoted:

"Science without religion is lame, religion without science is blind."

I lived in the desert most of my life. Now I live where there are trees and wildlife. I love to watch squirrels, and have been trying to lure them into my yard. At first there was no sign of them anywhere. But I kept putting food out. And water. Eventually we would see one passing through. Then there was one who stayed. Then two. Then three. Now there are usually some around. They disappear instantly when I go and put out their food. But then I can go into the house and know they will be there within the hour, enjoying it. Now I am going to start rubbing my scent onto the corn and seeds I leave for them so that they will know me in the only way they can. Learn to trust me. At any rate, associate my smell with their daily food.

But I want more from these nervous little furry creatures. I am going to put their food closer and closer to my house, then by my doors and windows. Then in a set spot where they can always come to look for it themselves. Maybe someday they will even take it right out of my hand. It's my goal; it's what I hope for. But I won't go out and trap them and bring them in. I won't bludgeon them so that I can own their soft fur and pet it any time I want. No, it is their trust and curiosity that I want. And for them to have their needs met. I want them to know me.

Just like God, the patient author of everything, tames us, His lost wild things.

Humility is what we need to seek from God. The ability to bow before a mystery, the willingness to ask and keep asking, the admission we cannot know everything. God is not trying to trick us, punish us. He is trying to *save* us, prepare us to live with Him forever. What matters is that we *seek* Him, not that we win our vain little debates.

Hell is full of people who always thought they were right.

The End:

THE LAST LESSONS

My Story

Daisy

He loved me. I thought it must be okay. But none of my school friends knew about sex stuff yet. Why did I? The darkest part of the secret was that I liked it. And hated it. And snuggled up next to it in other men and boys. Familiarity. The sick excitement.

I often showered with him. Where was my mother? Why was she never there? Didn't she know?

I finally told someone. But they never looked at me the same way again. So I learned to just keep everything to myself. Swallow the tears. Smile.

He gave me everything. Took me everywhere. Yet I was ashamed to share his name. The love itself was pure. Everything else a complicated blur.

Then stunned horror to see him do it to others. And sickened to discover most of the town knew. Alone at the end of his life, only one business partner at his bedside while dying.

How to separate the love from the perversion? How to find the nugget of love in my own life?

Only in the innocent children I protect with my own fierce, ruined love. Alone.

Chapter Ten

GOD OR SANTA

Praying vs. Begging

I have been driven many times upon my knees by the overwhelming conviction that I had nowhere else to go. –Abraham Lincoln

Once we have our faith growing, one of the next things we learn about God is what He is *not*. We always need to know the *real* person we are in a relationship with.

When I was seven or eight years old, my mother gave me a birthday party with school friends and a pretty cake. Then she told me that we were going to let the kids give me presents but we would give those presents to the local Children's Home.

I can remember most of the gifts like it was yesterday. Especially the one I really wanted to keep—a cloth pillow doll with very long legs. I carried it everywhere, already sad it would be leaving me. I never said anything to anyone about it. I could tell the other kids' moms admired us for doing it. But carried a heart-deep knowledge that it had nothing to do with *me*.

And mostly, in my life, none of the gifts I got ever had much to do with what I *wanted*. They mostly had to do with what others wanted to give.

But when I was turning sixteen, my mother answered my heart's desire: she gave me something that I actually wanted for myself and for no other reason than I wanted it. A pink suede cape. I can smell that distinctive leather smell and see the bright hot pink in my mind's eye as clearly as if it was yesterday. It is the only gift I remember from all the years of birthdays and Christmases.

So, like so much of life, my crooked journey to prayer was rooted in childhood. Never sure what was ok to say, to ask for. Confused about "blessings" (aka, "gifts") in general. Afraid to set myself up for disappointment. Yet yearning always for Love to give me what I really *wanted*.

And always, at bottom, a dread that if I didn't get it, they must not love me. Convoluted untruths based on childhood rejection, sure. But a pattern you don't expect to show up as an adult learning to talk to God. No matter where we started out in life, our prayer life is probably going to echo those early years.

SO, HOW CAN WE HEAR GOD?

I can still remember my first feeble attempts many years ago, in a darkened clothes closet. I had started reading the Bible, studying it with friends, maturing in my childish faith for the first time. But when it came time to actually talk to God, I was shy. Not even sure if I should address Him as "God" or "Jesus" or even "Sir."

I tried them all out that day, in that dark closet, my children playing in the other room. "God, Sir," I started out. "Jesus," once I knew more about Him. And yes, embarrassed that I didn't already know.

And He met me there in the dark as I began to see things from the tiny crack of light under the door and he whispered to me that I could not make my eyes open and "see" any faster, nor could I make my spirit. That all I had to do was share my heart with Him and He would then share His with me.

And it soaked in and He "showed" me things in my soul. Ways to hear what He wanted me to think, do, choose. I remember like yesterday touching my own ears and crying to Him, "I see!" and feeling His gentle "nod" in my spirit. I knew, from then on, that hearing from Him was as simple as *wanting* to, *choosing* to, being still and listening.

And understood that it wasn't going to be *audible*, not "heard" with my physical ears. "Heard" in my soul. The rest grew from that, because, frankly, there was no one else I trusted enough to ask back then.

Eventually, we see for ourselves that scripture helps us know Truth from lies. And *results*, too. But at the time, when we ask, it is the *peace* in our mind and soul. A "fruit of the Spirit" scripture says. Yes, and a talent we develop with practice.

A lot of us have secrets buried deep in our hearts. Our soul opens slowly, like a tightly folded rose. When God deems it safe to show us, we sometimes find we have been mad at Him for a long time. Maybe we blame Him for our lives not turning out like we hoped. Or wonder where He was when the Bad Thing happened. Maybe we even quit praying, leave the spiritual journey entirely, when our prayers aren't answered our way. This ol' fallen world sure supports *that* way.

Maybe—I confess here—even throw a little fit, have a little pity party, when we don't get our way. It happens. Life is hard, whether we are happy pilgrims or not. Our flesh continues to want what it wants, health breaks down, circumstances disappoint. And no one else to blame. Our first prayers do not bring what we asked right away. Even Santa only comes once a year. Sometimes we give both up in disappointment.

For a long time, I thought I needed to dream up what was best for me then *beg* God for it. It didn't seem to work. Slowly, I came to see that is not what "prayer" is at all. Not even a "conversation" at that level. Just begging. No room to trust His plan instead of my own. Which, if we think about it, is like a baby trying to tell mommy how to mix his formula from the crib.

Mommy knows what baby cannot know yet. We have to trust God to know more than we do.

There's no use pretending. He knows our hearts, even if we have somehow managed to fool ourselves, our friends. We are not giving Him information He didn't already have. But He is using it to build the relationship with us we both longed for all along.

ANOTHER HERO

There are a lot of heroes in the Bible. But my personal favorite is a sad little man who lost everything and still trusted God--Job. Oh, he wept and despaired and wondered why o why. Like we do. His "friends" came and told him where he must have gone wrong. His wife told him to curse God and die. But Job knew he was nobody to question the Lord God who made the universe. He accepted God's will in all things, even his immense suffering and loss:

> *The Lord gave and the Lord has taken away;*
> *may the name of the Lord be praised.* (Job 1:20)

"In all this," scripture goes on, *"Job did not sin by charging God with wrong-doing."* He could have. Like we so often do. Finally, God came Himself and told Job's doubting friends "Where were you when I formed the world?!?" and restored Job's fortunes.

Hundreds of years later, the apostle Paul summed it up in case they had missed it:

But who are you, a human being, to talk back to God? Shall what is formed say to the one who formed it, "Why did you make me like this?" Does not the potter have the right to make out of the same lump of clay some pottery for special purposes and some for common use? Romans 9:20-21

Humility before God is a good thing. We bow down in the dark and only then can see Him work. And it isn't usually instant. No more than our eyes can see anything in a dark room at first.

Yesterday, as I was writing this, I had a pleasant morning of work and freedom to think my own thoughts. I had no plans to go to church. But about the time I would have gone, I began to feel tearful. The burdens and losses of my family washed over me and sadness gripped me. Their lives were not what I had dreamed for them. I asked the Lord, in my Spirit, if He wanted me to go to church. An image flooded my mind, a smiling Jesus holding my face like a small child's. So I went, not because anything in me wanted to, nor because I was afraid not to. Only because my Lord, my best friend, brother and Hero, had invited me to, with love.

I cried all the way there, all during services. All the inner turmoil and fears and sorrows finally coalesced into one prayer: "Bless my family, Lord." I begged Him to let me stand in the gap for them where they might have missed His best. To let me bear the sorrow for where I failed them. Then, finally, towards the end, just "Bless them, bless them, bless them."

The communion wafers in our church now are small rounds, plus one large round they break and serve the pieces. Most everyone receives a small round wafer as the Lord's body. A few receive broken pieces that are mixed in. There is a folk tradition that says if you receive a broken piece, it is a special blessing.

Yes. My smiling Lord fed me that day with the broken piece of blessing. And whispered to me in my spirit how much I was loved, even though I could scarcely believe it. And how He covered my children too. It was both humbling and holy. I tear up even now to remember His sweetness, His gentleness. No matter how hard life is, I never get over the delicious consolations of being loved. Love covers the sorrows of life, then changes them, then makes them holy.

The reason I share something so intimate is because this is where so many stop short of receiving the full blessing of knowing God, trusting Him, loving Him, communicating with Him. We grow up thinking of Him as "the guy upstairs" or an old man with a long white beard. More like a mythical Santa, really, to ask for stuff.

No. Not even.

When I was a girl I went to bed and watched moon beams out my window and thought about God. Now I play games on my phone until sleep overtakes me. We have so many expectations about God, yet so little actual time with Him in this frantic world.

Then, we wonder why we don't get "yes" answers to all our half-hearted little prayers. That He doesn't always do what we ask Him to do. And sometimes we wonder why we bother.

When we develop that holy prayer relationship, though, we learn a lot of things, one important thing being what a relationship with God is *not*:

He is NOT a Hot Dog Stand.

You don't put in your order with God and He gives it to you your way. I mean, I like hot dogs, and am glad there's a stand where I can get one. But I do not *love* the hot dog vendor. I do not want a *relationship* with him. I have no loyalty to him; I'd just as soon get my hot dog at another stand. And he sure doesn't care about me, what might be best for me and mine.

It is NOT a club where you can hang with like-minded individuals, so you can feel you "belong." Churches are His plan alright, but we can miss His best there sometimes too.

It is NOT a Vegas act where you can be entertained. Nothing wrong with good message, good music, air conditioning. But Jesus isn't something that needs to be sold, like toothpaste. He is Someone to be worshipped in the deep stillness of our souls.

He is NOT a university symposium to air out theological gymnastics, hold forth with intellectual prowess. We can be very smart and still very lost.

Above all, God is NOT Santa.

No. The gospel, really good news, is so much deeper and more profound than that. A mystery so simple and yet so deep that mystics and children glimpse it best. An invisible door opens a bit, and blinding light of such beauty we cannot bear it stabs out at us. We see the puke bowl of this world and catch a glimpse of the original version that was made for us before we ruined it.

A Truth so deep that **we** are changed *even if our circumstances aren't*.

Our relationship with God is meant to be a love relationship.

Love so perfect that we will follow it in faith even when we suffer, even when we don't get what we want all the time.

Where we become something more than spoiled children; we become *divine* children.

Jesus is the complete embodiment of what God Himself had in mind for us. Perfect man, perfect God. We inherit all of that by association and adoption. We get it all because we are His. We walk—baby steps or strides—and learn. Learn that we are loved, that we can trust Him.

That we will do for Love what we simply will not do for fear.

There is a young wife and mother from our church who was brain damaged years ago in a car wreck. She has to live in a nursing home because her physical needs are many, and she cannot speak or tend to herself. But many visit her and all are deeply moved by her sweet spirit and smile. In spite of everything, if you ask how she is, she smiles and gives a "thumbs up" with her only working hand. Many take their prayer requests to her because they sense she is faithful to pray, joyful to do it.

Often those prayers are answered. Always she is the "talk of the town." Everyone who meets her is moved by her faith and joy more than by her handicaps.

There are all sorts of physically challenged people famous for their testimony. Helen Keller could not see or hear, but once she learned to communicate in spite of that, people flocked to her, bought her books, and interviewed her. She testified to the glory of God and people were moved.

Joni Eareckson was paralyzed when young, from the neck down, so she learned to draw and paint with tools in her teeth. Also famous, revered...her Christian testimony an inspiration to millions.

When we are broken physically, mentally, emotionally, people wonder, hint, or rudely say "If God is there, like you say He is, why doesn't He fix you?" We might begin to think we have nothing to offer as testimony because it "didn't work" for us.

Or, in church, they sing hymns like "now I am happy all the day....." And you wonder why *you* aren't happy all the day now that you know Jesus.

Well, Grasshopper, it is the biggest misunderstanding in Christendom since "name it and claim it." People want to think they can use God to their advantage and that is why they seek Him. That is one of the things the world has got *upside down*. If that is the only reason you chose to believe in Jesus, you are no different from those who believe in the devil for the same reason.

Did Jesus say "Blessed are the perky, pretty, and prosperous"?

No, He did not.

He said "Blessed are the meek, the poor, and the persecuted."

Did He say if you believed in Him life would be a bed a roses?

No He did not. He said we would "participate in the fellowship of His suffering."

No one would dream of saying to Joni, "God can't *use* you until He *heals* you, until you can *walk*." But they indicate all the time, "If this God you are so crazy about is so great, why are you depressed/ill/sad/broke/addicted/poor"?

If you are a misfit because you are poor or crippled or mentally ill, take heart. It is not *you* who has somehow missed the deep mystery of the "gospel." It is the *world*. You are closer to the heart and mystery of Jesus' mission than anyone.

If you are plain, deformed, toothless, homeless or lame, take heart.

If you love someone who the world discounts or demeans, learn from them, thank God for setting your heart near theirs, so you can see the kingdom in their purity of heart, their suffering.

A SAINT YOU'LL NEVER HEAR OF

The Bible says all of us true believers are "saints." And some churches recognize well-known ones and pay them extra honors. But there are many we won't ever know about here in this fallen world.

Let me tell you about a saint I know from the streets. Born a hermaphrodite-- physically, both male and female. Abused sexually and psychologically by a violent father. Diagnosed as Schizophrenic. Lived in mental institutions and on the streets. Now identifies herself as a woman in spite of the stubble of beard and gangly height. Nearly toothless from years of neglect.

And yet the Lord is her shepherd. She has a peace and generosity of spirit that is downright holy. And gratitude! Weeps for joy for a favorite song. Prays "Lord, bless us, we love each other" over a hamburger lunch. And the rest of us are moved to tears. Her path in this world has been stony and hard. But she will be one of the "lesser" who will be "greater" in Heaven, I'm sure. We are blessed for having known her, having held her hand in prayer.

Yet the world makes wide circles around her in the street.

Shame on the world.

When I was 2, I wanted to take off the hot plastic pants I wore over the soggy wet diapers.

When I was 8, I wanted the Miss Elizabeth doll with the tiny shoes and purses and bride gown.

When I was 13, I wanted a pink and black motorcycle and matching pink and black outfit.

When I was 17, I wanted a hot pink suede cape. And a boyfriend.

When I was 21, I wanted a job that didn't scare me.

When I was 23, I wanted to have a big wedding.

When I was 30, I wanted to travel.

Not *one* of those things do I want anymore. Some were blessings, some just adolescent ideas. Some were fulfilled, some weren't. Some made my life better, some nearly tanked it.

I'm just sayin'...we always *want* stuff. Sometimes we even *get* it. But we never know what's *best* until *later.*

But if we choose to trust God to love us enough to do what's *best* for us, even when we don't know what that is, we grow up and "get" it. Probably for the first time. Talking to Him about it is blessing enough, "gift" enough.

Life has a way of humbling us, doesn't it? Of happening to us while we've made other plans. And God has a higher idea for us than we do for ourselves. His is "forever," while we can't even delay gratification an hour.

We *need* those dark places we do not understand. "Via Negativa." The "negative way." Our *idea* of something can block our understanding of the *real* thing. *Not* knowing opens the way. When we learn to trust Him, we gradually come to see that understanding is not what is needed. That it is, in fact, overrated. We need to have *faith*--in the only lover of our soul.

Jesus Himself said that He was the "shepherd" and that His sheep knew His voice. Yes. Just like that. For years I mostly talked *to* Him. Then I gradually learned to *listen*. Now it is the deepest, surest pleasure of my life to listen, even when I have no words to say to Him. He understands our "groanings, too deep for words." (Romans 8:26)

That is the way any "relationship" grows. You spend time with the other person. You share yourself. You ask them to share themselves. You listen.

And that is how our relationship to God/Jesus/Holy Spirit grows as well. We spend time with Him, learn His ways. He is our *Abba*, our "Daddy". We can trust His love. Whether blessed or chastised, answered "yes" or answered "no."

No namby pamby thing, this faith. Not tra-la-la, now I am happy all the day. No Santa Claus, waiting for a list of wants. But a deep soul conviction that the true and the good and the beautiful are in Him. We *believe* God's love, even when we cannot *feel* it.

Then we know the *real* that will last *forever*. Not just the *notion* that comes once a year.

Patricia

My mother was my world. I have no memories from early childhood without her in them. When I was five years old I remember standing beside her outside, holding her hand while she talked to someone in the dark parking lot. The scratchy leaves of the boxwood along the sidewalk made me look down. Then there was a boom and flash of light. And my mother fell at my feet, still clasping my hand.

Running feet, yelling, car doors slamming. And my mother would not get up.

Now grown up I cannot tell my own story because I do not know who I am. Other people tell me I am like this or like that. Tell me things I do not remember saying or doing. One friend tells me when I get nervous my pupils go tiny and my voice changes. She calls it "multiple personality disorder." The doctor calls it "dissociative identity disorder." It doesn't make any difference to me what they call it because it never changes anything.

I am kind, others are mostly kind back. But I stay back a bit because I don't know who or what will be next.

I only know I miss my mother. Shot dead by my side one night many years ago by a boyfriend outside in the parking lot.

And I only trust God to put the puzzle back together someday.

Chapter
Eleven

BROTHER ASS

The Only Donkey We Have

We are not human beings having a spiritual experience; we are spiritual beings having a human experience. DeChardin

The other big thorn in the side on our journey is often our body. Even the most spiritual mystic finds himself on the toilet with cramps or hacking up a lung with the flu. We spend huge chunks of time thinking of the next meal or trouble with our bowels. The vast majority of every prayer list going around every group is requests for physical healing. It is the insistent yammering of this, our "Earth Suit," that most easily derails our desire to look *upward*.

"Brother Ass," St. Frances called his body. Stubborn donkey. I must concur.

Tell your body "no" and it whines for a sweater or a fan, chocolate or coffee or wine. Tell it "yes" and it eventually tires and disappoints, sometimes with scars.

Even people whose bodies no longer operate properly are stuck with its demands. A quadriplegic's nose still itches; an amputated leg is still plagued by "phantom pain."

And we all see the sweet spirit within our "special needs" people, but wonder how the Lord lets it happen, how to serve Him anyway. Wonder how some of us even manage to get through our journey to faith with the bodies we've been dealt.

And probably the majority of us wonder why we aren't quite like others. The World is selling beauty, fame, success all the time...makes us wonder why we are "different" or why we can't be "better."

I saw a television documentary once of a severely brain-damaged young man, blind, palsied, unable to speak or walk. His aging mother carried him on her back from place to place, taught him to play piano. Loved him, fed him, and taught him the gospel. Most of the program was narrated by the interviewer, asking questions of the sweet little mother herself, not really including the young man as he was known to be incapable of speech.

But at the end of the interview, the narrator did turn to the young man and ask: "What does '*love*' mean to you?

He struggled to the piano bench, leaned his head back, face toward heaven, and played "Amazing Grace" as beautifully as I've ever heard it played. I cried and nodded to our Lord.

Some of my Beloveds struggle on their journey because the mother who raised them was bipolar. Others because *they* are themselves. Some never conquer obesity, or arthritis, or scoliosis or mental glitches. Find their lives colored by their physical defects every day.

I had a precious friend once who said she had "Multiple Personality Disorder." I never believed in that myself, until I knew her. Thought it was something dreamed up for movies or books. But no. She became a stranger to us when under any kind of stress. Her pupils became pinpoints, the eye contact lost in a stunned stare. Body rigid and voice different from the one we were familiar with. This break was how she stayed safe. And it was the thing that ruined her for the world.

She was a kind and empathetic person, easy to talk to, funny, never judged. She could remember everything about that day when she was five years old and held her mother's hand outside by a parking lot. Remembered her mother arguing with a man. Remembered the loud bang that startled her until she trembled. Remembered looking at her mother's dead bloody body on the ground.

It took more than one person to hold all that pain. "Dissociative Identity Disorder." Those of us who knew her knew. And understood.

OUR BODY, OUR TEMPLE

There are a million ways our bodies—our "Earth suits" through this life—fail us, disappoint us. Tick tock tick tock, the stomach growls, the grass grows, the head aches, the nose runs. Science has proven that the traumas and stresses change our actual brains.

Scripture says our body is the "temple of the Holy Spirit." Which is too lofty for me...mine doesn't feel worthy. But it is the only donkey we *have* to ride on this journey of faith. So we take care of it, hope it will get us there. We do the best we can. But we must never be duped by the millions of lies the world is telling us about its importance. It is just a vehicle. If it isn't perfectly beautiful or healthy or fit, it is still where God's Spirit dwells for our mission here on Earth.

There are several design "flaws" I intend to bring up with the Lord someday: Why couldn't he have made teeth removable? The dentist would be a wonderful thing if it was a shop where you could drop them off. And why is the place we swallow our food right next to the place we take in air? Choking is an ever-present danger.

Which is not to mention the unfortunate placement of our private parts--life creating functions laughably close to excretory ones. It's almost as if our Creator wanted us to be humble, not take ourselves too seriously.

He must have His reasons for leaving us here in our "Earth Suits" before we are freed to live with Him without them.

Maybe to learn to walk by faith. Or the spiritual virtue of humility. Maybe our "forever" is being worked out by our choices here in the desert. Maybe it is just part of the fabric of the universe that He will not tear. We cannot know. We can only have faith. And faith does not mean faith in *us*, in *our* faith. It means faith in *His* reasons, even though we cannot know them. Faith in His love. Faith means accepting that our finite little brains cannot possibly hold the whole truth, but accepting that His does.

Have you seen the photos taken by the Hubble telescope?! Stare at those and tell me you think you could grasp the whole truth now. And then tell me you would want to float out there forever, without being held by anything larger than yourself.

Scripture has a lot to say about these fragile vessels and their holy potential:

> *...we have this treasure **in earthen vessels**, that the surpassing greatness of the power may be of God and not from ourselves; we are afflicted in every way, but not crushed; perplexed, but not despairing; persecuted, but not forsaken; struck down, but not destroyed; always carrying about in the body the dying of Jesus, that the life of Jesus also may be manifested in our body.*
> (2 Corinthians 4:10)

During my own physical suffering, I often begged God to change me, disappointed, even angry, that He didn't. I was sure that it meant there was something I was missing, or that He didn't like me. Maybe I didn't have enough faith. *Something.* Then, after many years of it, a lot of studies, a lot of prayers, He let me see—just a little—into His unfathomable mystery.

A mental image of myself, shackled to a wall, in pain. My first thought was "Yes! That is how it feels! Like I am a prisoner, being tortured, but I cannot escape."

Then, panning down the image, I saw the molten horrors of the things His shackles had *saved* me from below. The suffering in my flesh was His best way of keeping me safe from where I had been headed *before* He saved me. It may not mean to you what it meant to me. But it was vivid and true and has stayed with me ever since. Once we give our lives to Him, He will do whatever it takes to keep us in His best will. And maybe it will *cost* us something. Might be suffering. Might be our life. But He promises to protect our eternal *soul*.

I still struggle with my donkey flesh. Would have it another way if I could. Paraplegics sometimes curse God because they can't walk. The blind or deaf or paralyzed will be tempted to do as Job's wife urged him—"curse God and die." But when we remember what we are nurturing here, in this raggedy old Earth Suit, is our *Spirit*, then it does not control our life. This old disobedient, whiny, scared, depressed, painful, addictive, selfish, angry flesh won't survive transport, for which we will be—literally—eternally grateful.

WHAT ABOUT CRAZY?

They say "mental" illness like it's in the imagination or morals. No. "Mental" illness is still old Brother Ass. Whether it got there by genes from birth, drugs, traumas from childhood, or crazy thinking from the devil, it affects the actual *brain*.

But you can still have the "mind of Christ." Medication can be a mercy of God. Counseling can help. Feeding your spirit with God's Truth helps a *lot*. Even St. Francis would have told you that. That was all he *had*, and it turned him from a spoiled brat into a saint.

Psychiatry has not had much to offer but medication and labels. I've known so many people saddled for life by the labels that were affixed to them: "Depressive, Neurotic, Manic Depressive, Cyclothymic, Borderline Personality Disorder, Anxiety Neurosis, Schizophrenic, Paranoid, etc. They talk like that defines you, that it is who you *are*.

No. No more than some are "asthmatic" or "anemic" or "chronic diarrhea" people. We are God's precious souls with kinda ratty flesh. Maybe your "Earth Suit" isn't very reliable. Brother Ass is stubborn and flea-bitten. But that is not *you*. And it is not *forever*. You *do* have to tend it, feed it, and respect it. But it is not your *identity*.

God doesn't use labels. He truly does love us *like we are*. He can help us find which medication, which counselor, even which friends and work and food and drink. He wants to help us get our needs met. Because He cares more for our relationship with Him than anything. Waits on us to ask. Does the most when we surrender.

He knows better than anyone what a corrupted, polluted place this earth is and how hard it is to live in it. The only point of even doing it, to my way of thinking, is to learn to walk in faith and love. Just as if we were fish and had to live in a toilet somewhere until our pond was ready.

Heaven *will* be a relief, no doubt about it. But there are things He wants us to learn and experience *here* first. We are not human beings having a spiritual experience...we truly are spiritual beings who are having a human experience. For reasons known entirely only to our Creator.

"Panic Disorder" was the only label medicine put on my main malady. And just in my own small circle of wounded friends and relatives there were two criminals, three alcoholics, two bipolar, and many maladies in between. Guess if you hit ten donkeys over the heads with mallets, they'd all do a little something different with their pain. All I know for *sure* about all of us and our problems is that God *loves* us. Right now, today. Whether we "get better" or not.

Starting from there, it is easier to deal with Brother Ass. Instead of wondering why God is torturing us, faith begins to ask how God can *use* our bodily woes, turn them to good. Turn our natural self-centeredness to His higher purpose. That is a large part of what He is saving us from--Self.

Augustine thought that sin *was* this self-centeredness, the soul turning in on itself—"*homo incurvatus in se.*" Like a black hole where things go in, nothing comes out, not even light. Holiness is loving God and others. Self-centeredness, self-absorption, is what keeps us *from* God. It is our "sin nature." You remember Adam and Eve, the instant they sinned, *knew* they were naked. When they had been naked all along. Their focus turned from God to Self.

Another flesh battle that is raging more and more today is *addiction*. Sex, drugs, alcohol, behavior patterns. Most of them entrenched in the physical body/brain in ways we are only beginning to understand. For ourselves, or for someone we love, we earnestly seek God for this more than anything besides illnesses or "special needs." It *is* a special need! And He is the only cure for it that I myself have witnessed.

Addictions are so personal and so painful, so deeply imbedded in the pathology of our early lives, that they are well guarded from the light of Truth. It's just not safe to divulge them. And yet we are, like they say "only as sick as our secrets." And only God promises to "set us free" with His Truth.

When we "use", it makes us numb to the pain. Helps us forget the pain and shame of our childhood, mostly. Protects us from judgment and rejection by others. It's our best friend, sad to say. *Real* friends might reject us or hurt us. It gives us something to look forward to that won't disappoint. And we just don't know how to *get* anything less harmful that will do all that for us. We don't think we can live without it. Just a momentary, weak-willed decision to try leaves us feeling lonely and abandoned and vulnerable and scared.

So many things we are addicted to nowadays, with our affluence and perverted media and free time and welfare safety nets. "Sex, drugs, and Rock n Roll" *seems* like a cool lifestyle. Until you live it. A young man we know and love told us with tears that he really would rather be *dead* than live that life. Yet he is still ensnared in it. His toxic father tells him straight out he *ought* to just kill himself. Can you imagine surviving that much pain without the numbing?

Sex is another area where our bodily urges betray us. A young friend once wrote me about her latest sexploits, and then confided: "I think I may have this problem with being addicted to sex from different guys..."

Well, sure she did. Bigtime. Like a lot of women. Next to drugs and chocolate, sex is the easiest feel-good dime out there. An easy source of affirmation (somebody *wants* me!) and a great little physical kick for the brain to bookmark and come back to later. It's just so darn fun and legal and all. But, like all addictions, it's a dead-end as a lifestyle. Hey, God *invented* sex. But He meant it to be a total committed package with someone who loves *all* of you.

And if there is anyone besides the Lord Himself who can teach us what perfect love is, I sure never heard of them.

So do not be dismayed when ol' Brother Ass disappoints you, betrays you even. Complicates your life choices. Flesh is flesh. So many ways it disappoints us for living in this world. It is just the donkey we ride into town. And know that those of us who have a kinda lame ol' donkey are usually even closer to our Lord.

He will hold your hand. (Psalm 37:24)

He will come for you, rescue you, even if no one else ever did. (Psalm 91)

SPOTTED PUPPIES

You don't have to be healthy, strong, or good-looking for God to love you, wait for you, hold you, and rescue you. All you have to do is *choose* to know Him, go to Him with your secrets and your pain. Stay on the mission in His name. Keep that stubborn donkey on the trail.

He doesn't expect us to be perfect in our bodies or brains any more than He expects us to be perfect in our souls all the time. He *knows* why we need a Savior.

I am so whiny and ungrateful and scared when I'm sick, I do not know why He even likes me. Or why the people I know do. But I cling, in my broken little way. And He always comes for me. The light at the end of every dark tunnel.

He will come for you too. Honestly? Scripture has a lot of evidence He likes us imperfect ones *best*.

When my dog had a litter of five puppies, they all were shades of brown, like her. Except one. He was spotted and tiny and not very strong. The runt. Brown and white like a guinea pig. I fell in love with it at first sight. Felt sorry for its tiny, needy, last-in-line runty self.

But the surprise was...so did everybody else! Every single person who stooped to look into that nesting box loved that little struggling one! That runty little spotted puppy who wasn't quite like the others. The one who had to wait in line while its stronger brothers and sisters nursed. Had to stay blind days longer than the rest, since their eyes opened first. Had to be last to struggle out of that six inch tall nesting box, when the others were out playing days before.

Everyone's favorite.

Do you see? God must love us spotted puppies best too, or we wouldn't be here, would we? So, if you need a little more than other people, hurt a little more, can't quite keep up sometimes? You have a special place in God's heart, I promise you.

I used to love watching that little spotted puppy whine and yelp to keep up with the others, do what they were doing. Falling back in defeat most the time. Slow to grow, needy and weak.

Guess what? He was "Pick of the Litter" to the father's owner too! And made the most beloved, beautiful pet of all.

So, if we are a little different, us misfits, we have a different, harder journey. But maybe a higher, holier one.

So be spotted, baby! Be who you are! Who you were made to be. And He will love you for it. Even turn it to good.

Speaking of problems with our ol' donkey flesh...the most popular blog ever published on the Patron Saint of Misfits site? *This* one...one way our body is a burden to many of us:

Who Put the "I" in Anxiety?!

None of us want it. A *lot* of us get it. 18.1% of the U.S. population--dang near one out of five people!—have a diagnosed anxiety disorder. The "silent epidemic" most of us keep more secret than hemorrhoids or "female trouble."

Panic Disorder

GAD (Generalized Anxiety Disorder)

PTSD

Social Anxiety

Labels abound. Fixes? Not so much. Pills of course...but with problems of their own. Therapy of all kinds. Some of which helps, but never *cures*.

Dang near every book in the Bible has a "fear not" verse in it. From Genesis to the gospels God tells His followers not to be afraid for He is with them. So we feel guilty when we still do:

> "Do not be anxious about anything, but in every situation, by prayer and petition, with thanksgiving, present your requests to God. And the peace of God, which transcends all understanding, will guard your hearts and your minds in Christ Jesus." Philippians 4:6-7

But a word study equates the words "fear" and "anxiety" more with "worry." And we *can* stop *worrying* with our free will choice. We give it up and leave it to Him.

But we *cannot* always stop *anxiety* can we? No. That bent nervous system goes on tapping whether we are worried about anything in particular or not. I often wish they would give it a new label..."NeuroConsternitis" or something.

And because it is *invisible*, the suffering is amplified. No wheelchair, crutches, cast or Band-Aids. Others can't *see* it, no lab test *shows* it, so most assume it is something *we* are doing wrong. Sympathy for a tumor or loss helps heal those victims. For *this* we hear "get over it" and "you're a mess."

If negative thinking and worry are the problem, then why does it wake us up at night too? We aren't worrying or negative-thinking *then*, are we?

Sure, we have become more sensitive to our body's signals over time. But a lot of our illness is *physical*, just like theirs. Our *brains* and *nervous systems* are *off*. Science has proven it can be *genetic*, identifying three known genes related to "Mood Disorder." Plus ample evidence it is partially toxins in our environment.

Some of us have a gene that will not process those toxins. There is a lot of new information about the brain all the time. And a lot they still don't know. But we do know our world is more stressful and polluted all the time. For many, that translates to what we call "anxiety."

Unreasonable fear.

Also, fMRI scans prove that childhood abuse damages the growing amygdala in the brain, home of the "Fight or Flight" reflex. So anxiety can be the skid marks the traumas of life left on our nervous system. I myself have a very scared two-year-old inside. Bad things happened when I was too young to fight. My "Fight or Flight" is permanently *stuck* on *flight*. That's what that adrenaline rush is. Worked for the cavemen running from tigers. Not so great for us today.

So, in a nutshell, anxiety is *not* all our fault. And definitely should *not* be our *secret* any longer! One out of five people?! No rare shame there, fellow pilgrims!

Even the apostle Paul had a "thorn in the flesh" he asked God to remove. It never happened. He accepted it and wrote three fourths of the New Testament.

> "...a thorn was given me in the flesh, a messenger of Satan, to harass me, to keep me from being too elated. Three times I besought the Lord about this, that it should leave me; but He said to me, "My grace is sufficient for you, for my power is made perfect in weakness." I Corinthians 12:7-9

I wonder if *his* thorn was anxiety? Like he says, it does slay pride and make us wise about the devil. Helps us lay our *fleshly* goals down so *God* can work *through* us. Fist bump, Paul! A very worthy goal.

So after many years of being blindsided repeatedly and doing *everything* the world offers and still suffering from anxiety, I finally decided to just *lay it down. Let* His grace be sufficient for me too. Would I trade with the lady who lost her only son? No. Or my friend who has a brain tumor? No way. Maybe with the girl who lost her parents and best friend in a car wreck she survived? Definitely not.

So "Lord thank You for this" is my pill now. I *offer it up* to the Lord who knows me better than I know myself. The gratitude brings a flush of spiritual consolation. And a way to thumb my nose at the devil's dark insinuations. It holds me closer to the Lord than I ever would have been without it.

Think about it. Who do *you* cling to most when you are scared you are dying? God.

Good company.

So that "I" in anxiety? *Nope.* Not all our fault. And we share the Lord's own sufferings when we have it. Jesus sweated drops of blood in that Garden! He begged God not to make Him do it. He got up and did it anyway. He knows! And *we* know it keeps us humble and leaning on Him.

So *thank* You for these hellacious sensations in our bodies, Lord.

The ones that keep us humble, skulking out of ERs and calling in to work.

That keep us looking *up.*

That teach us about Your faithfulness.

Thank you.

Maybe not while we are sobbing or taking our pulse at midnight or crying with fear we are dying.

But we do know, more than most, that we are entirely lost without You.

Thank You, Lord. Turn it all to good, Lord.

Thank You for the million mercies that come when the horror passes. It builds our trust.

Whew. Thank You.

"When I am afraid, I put my trust in you." (Psalm 56:3)

Emma

I think I know how Eve felt when the innocence of the Garden of Eden was ruined in one dark day. My brightest day and darkest day were both in the same year--my eighth. Eight years I had with a mother and a father and three siblings in the sepia tones of an old movie. Normal. Safe. Playing. Hugging. Knew enough about God to walk the aisle at church and receive Jesus as my Lord; followed Him in baptism. Walked the days in the sun as children do.

Then one day, when I was eight years old, my mother went to the store and my father laid on the couch watching TV. I crawled up on top of him to cuddle and watch with him. My Daddy.

He picked me up and carried me to the back bedroom and did what no child should ever know. I didn't know anything about all that. Yet I knew to be ashamed. Left the room and ran outside, crying. Rode my bike as far away as I could. My world dragged through into a darkness that lives in a corner of my heart many years later.

I learned a lot fast. Told mother, heard her ask him why. Heard him say "I always come home at 5:00." Which meant that it was her fault somehow for leaving me alone with him. I felt sorry for her, but never close to her. Never really secure with either of them again. Had to decide to be brave for myself, not take anything for granted.

Years brought rumors of other girls, my sister for one. Mother's sorrow. Daddy a Deacon at church. The confusion. At first I thought God didn't love me anymore. Didn't trust Him. But then saw myself laying in His arms and Him carrying me, pure. Like floating in water. And knew He did not judge me, knew He was the only safety, the only perfect love.

Nothing to do about other people and God's gift of Free Will. But He made me strong and I still am. Many years of surgeries for a brain tumor and the other challenges of life, my father's scars and my Lord's faithfulness are still the defining moments.

Over the years, the Lord taught me to love and trust Him in spite of everything. Made me braver than I would have been. Brave enough to scream "Get away from me!" when I was older and Daddy tried it again. Mother still defending him even as she lay dying years later.

I would never bring their grandchildren near them. The sad blur of ruined family life wove itself into my heart forever.

But always the peaceful arms of the Lord were around me, floating on the water.

Faith. In spite of everything. The mystery of Free Will, the poison of sin. The beauty of the only perfect love. His.

Thank You, Lord. In spite of everything, thank You.

Chapter
Twelve

BAD SAMARITANS

Understanding Your New Family

Another bump on the rocky pilgrim's path...other Christians.

First, A Little Humor About It All:

If it weren't for Christians, I'd be a Christian. -- Mahatma Ghandi

"I love mankind...it's people I can't stand." --Lucy, "Peanuts"

Tell me I'm doing good, I'll do better.
Tell me I'm doing bad, I'll give up. --Kitty Smither

Why do born-again people so often make you wish
they'd never been born the first time? --Katherine Whitehorn

People are self-centered to a nauseating degree.
They will keep on about themselves while I'm explaining me. --Piet Hein

If 666 is the number of the Beast...what is 668?
The neighbor of the Beast. (old joke)

**And my personal favorite jibe at the way we throw
rocks at each other's churches:**

"I was walking across a bridge one day, and I saw a man standing on the
edge, about to jump off. So I ran over and said 'Stop! Don't do it!' '
Why shouldn't I?' he said.
I said, 'Well, there's so much to live for!'
He said, 'Like what?'
I said, 'Well...are you religious or atheist?'
He said, 'Religious.'
I said, 'Me too! Are you Christian or Buddhist?'
He said, 'Christian.'
I said, 'Me too!
Are you Catholic or Protestant?'
He said, 'Protestant.' I said, 'Me too!
Are you Episcopalian or Baptist?'
He said, 'Baptist!'
I said, 'Wow! Me too! Are you Baptist church of god or Baptist church of
the lord?'
He said, 'Baptist church of god!'
I said, 'Me too! Are you original Baptist church of god, or are you
reformed Baptist church of god?'
He said, 'Reformed Baptist church of god!'
I said, 'Me too! Are you reformed Baptist church of god, reformation of
1879, or reformed Baptist church of god, reformation of 1915?'
He said, 'Reformed Baptist church of god, reformation of 1915!'
I said, 'Die, heretic scum,' and pushed him off."
--Emo Phillips

I'm with Ghandi on this one. Christians can be a prickly lot.

We are the best and the worst advertisements for the faith. We provide more help to the poor, sick, and downtrodden than the government or Red Cross. Yet we aren't perfect and can be pretty poor advertisements for the faith.

Mostly by the way we criticize wounded misfits for their "sin problem" when they have come seeking the mercy and grace to help them overcome those Band-Aids they've put on their wounds.

And more all the time because of the way many denominations throw rocks at other denominations. Someone on the outside looking in? Yeah, that would make them less likely to enter *any* of them. How could they trust God if none of his "family" agree on His "rules?"

Years ago, I gave up on church altogether for a while. Too much sniping, too many ways of saying I had it wrong. Then I met Maria. She cleans houses. She told me about her ornery church friends making her life miserable. I told her about mine.

Then she told me about when her beloved son died of cancer and she didn't even have enough money to bury him. Already sick and hollow with grief, she just cried out to the Lord. By that night, people from her church, many of them strangers, had individually stopped by with gifts of cash totaling $6500. The exact amount she needed for a lovely service and burial for her son.

And that's what church is for. People, sick and well, gather to worship, stay to minister to each other. Doing it *wrong* until they learn to do it *right*. Always new ones coming in, just starting out, not fully formed.

Jesus knew it:

> "It is not the healthy who need a doctor, but the sick. I have
> not come to call the righteous, but sinners." (Mark 2:17)

We shouldn't be so surprised church folks don't always have it right. It was that way from the start. New Christians have a lot to learn. And we bring a bundle of old flesh patterns with us. My friend John thinks we should be locked up for six months after we are saved, before we offend anyone with our zeal or ignorance.

And some can become overly impressed with all they've learned and become pretty full of themselves. We still use the ancient word for the first religious know-it-alls: *Pharisees*. And Phariseeism is still an occupational hazard of all religious people.

When a lost and wounded person becomes a Christian, is he instantly perfect?

No.

When a sick person walks into the doctor's office, is he instantly healed?

Never.

BEHAVIOR POLICE

The first churches put baby Christians through three *years* of discipleship before they allowed them to receive the sacraments of the church. Taught them the rudiments of the faith. Demonstrated by their service the love and humility of mature faith. Washed their feet. Taught them scripture, prayers, sacrificial giving. How to be a part of the body of Christ and a local community of faith. We don't always get that today. We mostly just walk the aisle or sign a paper.

Mainly, we forget that everybody needs *love* more than they need *behavior police*. Sometimes it seems like the Lord gave us a lavish banquet of delicious warm food, and we all walked in and started throwing it at each other...accusing each other of eating wrong, sitting wrong, talking wrong.

And, even if they mean well, when all someone seems to want is to "fix" you, it is the same as them saying "you are not quite right."

But sometimes we share our own brokenness with others, make it safe for them to share theirs. And that becomes a true *community* of faith. We experience what the Lord Himself prayed for in John 17: "...protect them by the power of your name, the name you gave me, so that they may be *one* as we are *one*."

All the icky kinds of religiosity come from starting with *behavior*. You know...the *rules*. True Christianity, becoming a bondservant of Jesus, starts with *Him*. That love relationship with Him changes us. Then we *want* to change our behavior, work in His vineyard. He loves us first, we love Him back, and then we want to please *Him* more than our own selfish desires. Slowly, gradually. Not instantly. Just like children growing up.

So there are always pilgrims along the road at every stage of formation. Pilgrims who might hurt your feelings. Other pilgrims who are not yet perfected in Love. And pilgrims who hold you, feed you, pray for you, love you through the death of a loved one, the horror of a wreck, and all the hurdles of Life. Pilgrims who give their time and money and prayers to hospitals, orphanages, twelve-step programs, schools, children all over the world. Who help with the milestones of marriage and burial. Your new "family" in the Lord.

Running soup kitchens, feeding the homeless camped out under the bridge, taking communion to the homebound, sooo many ministries meeting needs in our society. The last church we joined had 84 distinct ministries you could sign up to participate in.

Yet no other group calls down such animosity in the secular public. Nobody likes "religion" these days. Or "church," even if they are willing to believe in God. The public and the media say it's because of how Christians act. Says they are hypocrites.

213

But regular Alcoholics Anonymous members fall off the wagon all the time. Nobody shouts "Imposter!" at *them*. Nobody stays out of AA because of them. Nobody tells them they don't believe them. Or hates them. Nobody claims the whole program is worthless.

But let a *Christian* act bad and you'll see it in the evening news.

We have to accept that there are going to be some bad Samaritans along the way. *And that the other pilgrims are not who we are following.*

Even Ghandi was enamored of the gospel when he read it and studied it. He knew the Truth when he saw it, thought that Jesus embodied it entirely. But, when he looked at the people who claimed to *be* Christians, he stopped short.

We live a long way downstream from that cross. We Christians are not what we *could* be, any more than our churches are.

And some have had such bad experiences in a church that they've burned the bridge entirely. Abuse, criticism, weird doctrines or sermons. It happens. Because they are full of *other* sinners and misfits at every stage of spiritual development. With every kind of gift and every kind of wound. And the devil, of course, still roaming about like a "roaring lion," looking for some to devour or delude. (I Peter 5:8)

It can be confusing. The Bible does talk about the best way to *behave*, just like we instruct our children to stay out of the street, and for the same reason. Love. But then we drop back into separate camps and throw stones at other guys, in total defiance of His *main* instruction to "judge not."

In the workplace, some are offended by believers with misplaced zeal or flesh-driven desire to "reach others for Christ." Browbeating, even criticizing or condemning them to accept their own brand of doctrine or worship. Instead of *demonstrating* to them how much God loves them and how He enriches their own life. Making notches in their belt instead of disciples for the Lord. *Telling*, not *showing*.

214

Some people don't yet understand who they are *in Christ*, still define themselves by what they *do*, like lost people. The same prideful one-up-manship in a different environment, for whom "Bible knowledge" or "good works" are just another way to excel. We still have our flesh, and it wants to be *ahead*. It wants *credit*. It gets, as the Bible puts it, "puffed up." (I Corinthians 13:4)

And of course there's the crazies you read about in the newspaper. Cult leaders and pedophiles and adulterous pastors and worse. Doing hellish things and daring to name the name above all other names—Jesus. Ooooo, a special room in Hell for *them*.

You have to be, as scripture puts it, "wise as serpents and innocent as doves." (Matthew 10:16) Not throw the baby out with the bathwater. Anyway, why should we be so surprised? Didn't nearly every paragon of peace invite a violent end? Jesus, crucified, Martin Luther King, Jr., shot dead. The tumult, and downright *evil* at loose in the world truly does hate the gospel of love and peace.

HUMBLE HEROES

Make no mistake; there are also many humble heroes there we can count on to help us in His holy name. Who will pray for us, counsel us. People we can trust and love like true brothers and sisters as we share the faith journey. For some of us they become our "family." Give us what we never got in our birth families.

I remember working alongside one woman in a Christian camp for poor kids. She cooked all day to put out three meals, then, in the evening, as we all sat around exhausted, she rubbed other people's feet while we all chatted. I have forgotten every message preached at camp that summer. But I have never forgotten that foot rub.

It takes a long time to heal a soul. Anyone looking in the window could not see the slow, steady miracle of a soul growing, healing. Even surgery patients at the hospital have a faster turnaround.

And every single pilgrim along the way has a different wound in a different stage of conversion. Everyone who falls in love with our Lord brings their wounds with them when they start their own journey of faith.

When my youngest was about seven or eight, she argued with her big sister one morning over the belt she was wearing to school. Claimed it was *hers*, sister claimed it was *hers*. I didn't know for sure, so asked them to go to their rooms and pray. In minutes, she returned, belt in hand, to the room where her sister and I waited. "He says it's hers, but I can wear it today."

So funny. So precious. And so the way He wishes we could handle our differences. Just tell it like it is. Share your heart, your hope, your opinion. Then listen to His leadership.

P.S.—her sister agreed ☺

Then, too, there is a way to be a Christian *culturally*, by *inheritance*. Grandma was a Christian, and Mom and Dad, so I must be too. Usually a certain denomination. So a lot of lost people doing "lost" things and claiming they are "saved." When they have never truly encountered the Lord at all. Knowing a lot *about* someone is not the same as knowing them *personally*. God included.

Love is what we are doing here. We are growing in holiness all the time when we love those who hate us, betray us, make fun of us, ignore us, and gossip about us. You know...*sinners*.

Love them like Jesus loves us. It is the simplest, most direct way we can be like Jesus. Love sinners. That is how we take the battle to the front lines. Overcome evil with good. Become His bondservant in redeeming the world. His plan is simple and eternal:

"Love one another as I have loved you." (John 13:34)

Ghandi was such a smart man. And so gentle. But he *missed* it. Looked in the wrong *place*. There is only one place you can look to decide to be a Christian, and that is *Christ*. There are plenty of *bad* Samaritans, plenty of prideful ones. But only one Jesus.

Even the Apostle Paul didn't get it at first, persecuted the early church, and was there when they stoned the first martyr.

Then the Lord Himself knocked him off his high horse and revealed Himself to him on the road to Damascus. And the rest is history. Read his letter in I Corinthians, chapter 13—the "Love Chapter"—and tell me actually meeting Jesus didn't make all the difference to the world's most famous Pharisee!

During WWII, in occupied countries, some people hated their "sympathizer" neighbors only to discover later that they were hiding a whole family of innocent Jews in their basement all the time. This world is like the Nazi-occupied countries in World War II. We are held against our will by the "god of this world" and we eye each other suspiciously. But we cannot know what our neighbor is up against. Or what battle he is fighting. Or how he might be serving our Lord. God does.

Human nature being what it is, some Christians want to think ill of other Christians for not doing things their way. Lob grenades across denominational lines instead of take the Word to the lost. The denominational wars gone public have made doubters and seekers afraid of *all* of us, really. Why would I want to believe what Christians believe if they even accuse each *other* of being wrong?! I often wonder if *that* isn't the main thing keeping people *out* of churches these days.

When I went to the Baptist church, my dad was disappointed because he'd raised me in the Methodist. When I went to Pentecostal services my friends made fun of me for being a "holy roller." When we went to the Catholic church my evangelical friends thought we were "lost."

And, truthfully, there were some churches I went to that I thought were spiritually dead and some a little nuts. But I do know for a fact if you give your life and soul to the Lord *He* will lead you where He wants you. We come to *Him* first, then He sets us on the journey that is best for us.

I've had good friends with good reasons for hating nearly every denomination there is. One raised by a Baptist preacher who hates all things Baptist, another schooled by "mean nuns" who hates all things Catholic, another raised Pentecostal who walked away when they were never healed. But they all (we all) found ways to love and serve God where we ended up.

EVERYONE IS ENTITLED TO THEIR OWN JOURNEY

A million differences. Do you really think the Lord is mad at people who come to Him with a little different understanding of Him? Do any two people in this world understand *you* in exactly the same way? I have my own idea of which is "right," of course. But I also think everyone is entitled to their own journey. We are safe if we are with Him.

These days, when the tares ("weeds" in Bible Greek) have been growing in the fields for so long, it's getting harder to find the wheat. Yet God doesn't want us pulling up the tares. Nope...He just wants us to be His bondservants in whatever field He's planted us, until He comes (Romans 1:1).

Not convert the lost world to *your point of view*, but convert them to *Christ*. More by loving *example* than by words. "Preach the Gospel," Francis of Assisi said. "And if necessary, use words."

The next pickle we believers get into is that it hurts our feelings (i.e., *pride*) when nonbelievers make fun of us. We hear the talk show hosts chit chat with a sarcastic edge, acting like faith is a sign of low IQ, in spite of the fact that the most brilliant minds in the world have been believers. The Bible is matter-of-fact about that, too:

> *Jesus said, "I praise You, Father, Lord of heaven and earth, that You have hidden these things from the wise and intelligent and have revealed them to infants.* (Matthew 11:25)

So what do we do? He says to "Count it all joy:"

> *Consider it pure joy, my brothers and sisters, whenever you face trials of many kinds, because you know that the testing of your faith produces perseverance.* (James 1:2-3)

Since we don't get martyred for our faith much in this country (yet!), we can find joy in the secular persecution by unbelievers. Smile when they make fun of us, put a nugget of joy in our bank when they scoff. It is what it is, and He warned us.

Germany called itself "Christian" and went along with Hitler, killed twelve *million* people in concentration camps. But we also know there were many true believers, devout Jesus bondservants, who died trying to correct this great wrong, trying to save people from the camps. Corrie Ten Boom ("The Hiding Place"), Dietrich Bonhoeffer, Father Maximilian Kolbe....so many more.

So, yes, some of the Christians we meet will be too arrogant or too timid, too pushy or not friendly enough, too rich or too poor. Some messages we hear preached will be boring, some too shallow, some too deep. Some of the "rules" will be God's, some man's. Some of the people we reach out to will not welcome us.

And some will humble us over and over with their compassion and faith-fulness. Be the family for us that maybe we never had.

Teresa of Avila's book, "The Interior Castle," describes the Christian's journey as an interior one. His soul progresses from an outer courtyard where he seeks conversion, but is easily distracted by things of the world. Then moves on to a deeper faith, more prayerful, increased learning. More open to the leading of the Holy Spirit within. Then experiences increased freedom from sin, is more charitable to neighbors, more mature in the faith. But still susceptible to temptations such as wealth or fame.

Thomas Merton described his own stages of growth as a *Seven Story Mountain*, in a book by the same title. It is an autobiography that tells of his progression over the years from pure intellectual pursuit of philosophy and narcissism, then communism, then entry into the life of faith.

Two classic Christian books describe the journey in allegory:

The Pilgrim's Progress, John Bunyan

Hind's Feet on High Places, Hannah Hurnard

Most of them boil our faith journey down to a path not unlike the development of a child:

1. Infancy: Observing, taking it all in, imitating others. Still completely Self-centered.

2. Childhood: Simple trust in what they are taught. Praying more, developing more a notion of who God is, but still doesn't know much scripture, no real opinions of their own yet. The "dress-up" stage.

3. Adolescence: Separating from others a bit, forming own opinions, but still accepting what they've been taught for the most part. Or rebelling against it.

4. Teenaged: Often a backward track, spiritually, as they seek their own way in the world. Making their own choices, perhaps seeing the evil in the world for the first time. Learning scripture, starting to apply it in their life. But fragile, susceptible to lies, false prophets, moonbeams and cults.

5. Young Adult: More rational and intellectual now, having learned some things the hard way. Knows more scripture, serves in Christian works, has a deeper prayer life. Unless broken by suffering or disappointment, might be self-righteous. But starting to truly love others rather than their own flesh desires. Beginning to see the struggle between Spirit and Flesh…learning to deny Self as they learn to walk in the Spirit.

6. Mature Adult: Walks in the Spirit more now, as opposed to living in the Flesh. Able to love, pray for, minister to others, even enemies, out of true love for the Lord and people, instead of a desire to look good to others. Brings others to the faith by their witness. The virtues of humility, kindness, patience, charity, self-control, purity become more incorporated into their default position, not such a struggle anymore. Christ is the center of their focus now.

No matter how you look at it, analyze it, there is one important thing to know: there will never be a time in this world where all the people in church are all renewed and Christ-centered at the same time. Where all are at the same point of maturity. Where all have stepped into the love and grace of God. But there are always *some*. If we cannot find the humble, loving sheep we had hoped to find, maybe we can *be* that kind for someone *else*.

As scripture points out: "Where two or more are gathered in My name, I am there in their midst." And He is. Broken people, perky people, shy and outgoing, rich and poor, all gathered in His name. The government might deign to send a needy person a check every month. But will they bring you a pot roast when you are sick? Take up a collection for your family when you lose your job? Pray for you when you lose a loved one? Comfort you, encourage you? Pray for you?

We might not always like the way other Christians act. They might not like the way *we* act. The only way around it is to love them in the name of the Lord of our lives—Jesus. We can do that. We need each other, brothers and sisters of the faith, for the same reason families do. Working out the "issues" every day. Learning to love and serve instead of scanning others all the time to see what they can do for you.

Maybe becoming more like Christ is, in fact, becoming more like *ourselves*. He made us like we are, put us where we are. Of course we are all different.

And churches are like watering troughs for horses--some kinda rickety, some big and stout. Some maybe even poisoned a bit.

But horses gotta drink. And cowboys gotta serve. "Church" is a new family where we give and receive, support each other, learn from each other. We misfits know.

And we know *Jesus* was a misfit *too*.

Church is not a nursery for saints, but a hospital for sinners. C.S. Lewis

...bearing with one another in love, making every effort to maintain the unity of the Spirit in the bond of peace. There is one body and one Spirit, just as you were called to the one hope of your calling, one Lord, one faith, one baptism, one God and Father of all, who is above all and through all and in all. (Ephesians 4:1-6)

Grace

I was left to the care of nuns in the hospital when I was born. They named me "Grace." A fitting name for a child who only had the Lord's grace to cling to her whole life. I never knew who my mother was and was passed to several homes while small.

The first trauma I experienced was so dark that I died from having the life pressed out of me by a man. Nameless, faceless, dark. Lifted up above myself, I saw but could not feel or speak. Then watched as I was carried from the floor and placed in my bed.

In my child's heart, I sensed an angel touch me, restore my life, and comfort me with peace.

I walked through many other trials with that same childlike faith and trust. I was never loved or cared for by humans in those early years. I remember only rejection, no bonds.

But I always understood, in my child's mind, that God was not responsible. Knew, somehow, that He protected me from the evil in the ones who were. And He always has.

So I learned to love because it was given to me by the One who *is* love.

Older now, I see that I am not alone. The Lord leads me to give to others with simplicity and love. Give what I only learned from Him, never had given to me. Some of us wounded children lean in closest to Him.

He knows.

He is eternally "enough."

God, who said, **"Light shall shine out of darkness,"** is the One who has shone in our hearts to give the light of the knowledge of the glory of God in the face of Christ. **But we have this treasure in earthen vessels, that the surpassing greatness of the power may be of God and not from ourselves; we are afflicted in every way, but not crushed; perplexed, but not despairing; persecuted, but not forsaken; struck down, but not destroyed;** always carrying about in the body the dying of Jesus, that the life of Jesus also may be manifested in our body. **Corinthians 4:10**

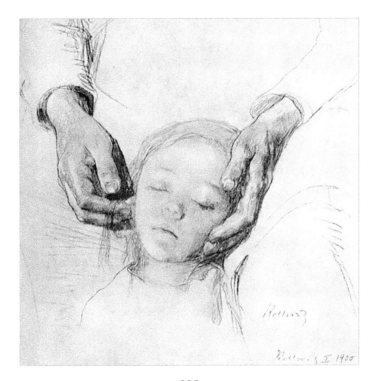

THE GIFT OF TEARS

Why Suffering?

God did the only thing He COULD do: He came in the
flesh and took His own medicine.
Dorothy Sayers

So now we've got the picture. What happened to us. What God did about it. The conflicts. The Hero. The Villain. Even our Superpower. The BIG story. OUR story, wrapped in His.

All the other lessons along the pilgrim's way make more sense to us than this one: *suffering*. We try to learn, accept, and be grateful anyway. But harbor that bitter *whyyyy* in our hearts. Wonder if it is *our* fault or *His*. It is the hardest stone on that rocky path of faith.

Working as a nurse in a large cancer hospital, I saw suffering of all kinds going all ways. Young then, I never realized how it was feeding my understanding of the "why" that haunts us when life gets so hard. Two of my own relatives helped it come clear years later.

My uncle we sat with while he lay in Intensive Care never attended church. But after being strapped down with a throat tube inserted quite a while we asked a pastor friend to visit him, pray with him. The pastor explained the Lord's salvation and grace and asked him if he would like to receive him. Tears welled in his eyes and my uncle nodded "yes." He received the Lord and was more peaceful for those last weeks of his life.

Finally, towards the end, after many days in a coma, lying flat on his back, too weak to respond or roll over or *anything*, he suddenly sat straight up, stretched both arms up toward the ceiling, eyes wide and staring up in awe. We knew right away. "Angels," we smiled at each other. The look of stunned joyous awe on his face was unforgettable.

When he laid back down he was gone. Peace in repose on his face.

On the other side of that coin was the slow, agonizing death of an aunt. An alcoholic her whole life, estranged from her children, divorced several times, she was the "black sheep" of the family. Hospitalized, intubated several times for emphysema, she struggled on.

Once, everyone was out of town except me, and I took her to the Emergency Room, barely breathing. The doctor, holding the respirator tubing in his hand, looked at me to decide if he should bother. We both knew she didn't have long to live either way. "Yes," I nodded, not willing to be the one to make that kind of decision.

They resuscitated her, put her in a room on a respirator. Days later, when they weaned her off of it, she was frantic to tell everyone her story.

"I left my body," she started, her voice still hoarse. "And floated in the room while they worked on me." Her eyes were gleaming with amazement. I was expecting the "tunnel of light" many patients describe as they lose consciousness.

But no.

"As I floated, I felt myself sinking downward, toward the baseboards." Her hand fluttered toward the floor of her hospital room, trembling. "And it was like a dark tunnel." She was wide-eyed, intense in a way I had never seen her. "It swirled down and down and was darker and darker." Tears filled her eyes, her hand circled and pointed downward.

Those of us listening moved in closer, caught in the unusual drama.

"And just as I was starting to sink down into the darkness, Hatch walked toward me, waving me away with his arms, saying 'go back, go back.'" She fought for breath, sighed.

She believed with all her heart that her ex-husband, "Hatch," had turned her away from the darkness. We were all speechless, but she herself begged for someone to talk to her about Jesus and Heaven. Too sick to go to church, she wanted to know everything.

For the last year of her life, she watched nothing but video sermons, asked everyone she knew to bring Bibles and books. Pastors visited. She became a different person before our very eyes.

Sometimes it takes a *long* hard road to make us pilgrims instead of wanderers. But it is apparently *never* too late.

DEATH…THE DEVIL'S GIFT

We know everybody has to die, but secretly hope an exception will be made in our case. It makes everything we do seem silly or grand. Because if we don't know anything else, we know we are going to die. We have all laid enough people in the ground to know that.

Death *is* the ultimate enemy. The curse the devil made. That was the price of that first fall in the Garden of Eden. And that is what we want saving from today.

We dash ourselves against the concrete seawall of mortality, but never win. We dress it up, laugh at it, hide it. But it remains the warp in the fabric of the universe. The bedrock of fear and futility under nearly everything we do.

And how are we supposed to fit all this into one loving God? The life, the death? The blessings, the curses? How did God overcome that one? How can we understand what He gave us in spite of it?

Only when we study Love. What love *really* is, not what the culture has reduced it to. Because God's love is ruthless. Not fuzzy bunnies and heart-shaped chocolates, but the hard reality of death and justice.

Not a lazy babysitter, watching us make our messes, thinking to clean up later rather than spoil our fun. No--a father who loves us too much to let us cross the busy highway.

He is more than simple kindness—He is a consuming fire, refining us so we can be pure gold.

We are infants in our cribs, totally dependent on Love to sustain us. Have you ever had to hurt a baby? Take them to the doctor for shots that make them scream in pain and betrayal?

Love knows things babies cannot know.

Misfits accept this more gladly because our hearts were already broken and what we feel or do not feel is forever out of our control. We are wounded and our feelings will just not line up and behave like everyone else's.

But God's love is not a *feeling*. It is a *fact*. A concrete yardstick set in the swamp of shifting moods and pain and confusion. It is the one sure thing. Not as a group or a race or a pair even, but each and every human snowflake. He desires a love relationship with each one of us that is unlike the one He has with *anyone* else.

God persists in wanting what is best for us in His "forever." We turn away, scream in pain, and reject Him for shaping us. But He keeps on shepherding us toward Him, so we can live with Him forever.

You'd think He would give up, since we've made it plain we'd rather do it our way.

WHY DOESN'T GOD JUST FIX US?

Often we wounded ones grieve about how we can't *do* more, *be* more. Why doesn't God *fix* us? Why aren't we joyful all the time? The "fruit of the Spirit" not for us? What are we doing wrong? For Christians, there are taunts from our secular world all the time. "Why praise God for surviving a wreck?" an ER doctor scoffed once. "Why did He let it happen in the first place?"

Why praise God for His faithfulness when you are crippled by a birth defect or mental illness? The lost world loves to point and sneer: *Where is your God now?*

Well, He is the same place He was for Job as he suffered and lost everything, and Abraham as he led the clan from everything familiar out into the desert. The same place He was when His only son was nailed to a cross. Read the Gospel of Mark, chapter 15. The crowd insulted Him, jeered: "Where is your God now? Come down from the cross!"

But He did not come down, because it was what He *came* for. And we would not be better, either, if we did not have the cross we have. Suffering, sadness, trials, circumstances are how we are being formed for eternity in a holy family. Our trials shape our *souls* every day.

A sweet Christian couple I know raised a son whose brain was severely damaged by a tumor in childhood. His speech is halting, his potential for employment limited. But he has an unmistakably sweet, pure, and capable Spirit. Quick to pray and earnest in faith. Of such as these, the Lord said, Heaven will be filled.

Everyone has something hard. Believers, doubters, haters, lovers...we hope there's a better world ahead, but right now we gotta get through *this* one. Dead animals in the road, people fighting and rejecting each other, addictions, illness, terrorists, lost children, death. I wish I wasn't like I am.

But I'm sure schizophrenics wish they weren't schizophrenic, and people with cancer wish they didn't have cancer.

I don't know anybody who doesn't wish *something*. It's a hard world.

At the same time, though, we are aware there are many hard things the Lord *hasn't* asked us to do. We feel bad to feel so bad. Ya know? I read the prayer requests scrolling by on church email—young mother of three with stage 4 breast cancer, paralyzed husband with pneumonia, car wreck that took the father and the child but left the mother, flood took the mother and two children but not the father, autistic child having surgery. On and on and on it goes, the suffering, the heartbreak, the sorrows of this world. We try to be grateful. Often fail.

Like the ancient Hebrew people, we want God to come and put a stop to our suffering. To make us happy, blessed, prosperous, powerful.

Instead, God Himself came down in the flesh and *shared* our pain. Jesus wept when His friend Lazarus died. He shed tears and drops of blood in Gethsemane, pleading Father God to save Him from what He knew was coming. The cross.

Scripture says we "participate in the fellowship of His suffering." (Philippians 3:10). But we sure don't *want* to.

If it cheers us up at all, Jesus didn't really *want* to, either, there at the end. He asked God the Father to "let the cup of poison pass" from Him. But no. Not to be. So He picked Himself up, brushed Himself off, and walked to His torture, suffering, and death.

"What soap is for the baby," a Yiddish proverb says, "tears are for the soul."

They are the silent words in our heart, for grief too deep to say. Scripture says God actually *saves* all our tears. (Psalm 56:8) They are a Holy treasure.

When you were a child and had a fever, you didn't think your Mother loved you because she made the fever go away. You thought she loved you because she stroked your hair and soothed you, brought you water, covered you up.

God's love is not manifested *less* because we suffer sometimes, but *more*.

It would have been so much easier, simpler, to write a sweet little inspirational book about something we suffered and how God fixed it. How we had cancer and He healed it, how we had drought, we prayed, it rained.

But we have to look Truth in the face: it often doesn't work that way. Sometimes there are miracles, often there are not. So what do we learn from that? Doesn't God love us? Isn't He good?

Let's just think outside the box for a minute here and ask ourselves: Why *not* suffering? There is so much of it. It is the *rule*, not the exception. Shouldn't the question, in this ruined world, be: *why are there islands of peace*? Why so much mercy? Why, really, when you ponder it, would God allow us to live to see another day at all?

We went to a blues concert once, and the band opened with a simple blues refrain:

"The Lord woke me up this mornin' "

Then a few bars of bass backup while we waited.

Then the singer leaned into the microphone and just said: *"He didn't have to."*

And the song played on. That one line is all I remember of the entire concert.

He woke me up this morning.

A new day, a fresh start, a deep love.

We forget the grace of every day and bemoan the setbacks. Our fallen nature remembers pain the best. Scientists today have proven our brains hold on to the bad longer than the good.

Why *wouldn't* there be suffering, given the way we behave? We hit our mommies, bite our friends, steal from our roommates, rape the innocent, and humiliate the good. We drink too much, eat too much, squander our money, cheat on our spouses, lie to our friends, and worse. Always thinking of ourselves. Sometimes we *deserve* to suffer for it.

If we are not too narcissistic or sociopathic to be blind to our bad deeds, we know perfectly well what we've done. You don't have to tell a drunk he's a drunk, for example. We remember where we've put parts of our bodies we shouldn't have, what we took that wasn't ours, the meanness we put out into the universe. The self-centeredness of our days.

We know. The big *lie*, then, isn't "God is good." The big lie is that *we* are good, when we know deep inside our soul that we are not. Not all the time.

Only then do we begin to love a savior. Someone who *is* good, who can save us from the darkness within. Who paid the price for our misdeeds, made us right with God the Father. Who can come alongside us, teach us, repair us, and make us His beloved child in spite of our fallen little ways.

We do crazy things to end our suffering. Look for something "more" that will make it all less painful or boring. Look for something to give it all *meaning*.

And there's the rub. It isn't the *suffering* that blocks our faith. Everybody suffers sometime. It is the fear that it has no *meaning*. That there are no more reasons for the *good* days than there are for the bad. That maybe our suffering is our judgment, our fault, that maybe God just doesn't even *like* us.

But no. I mean, dang... think what people did to *Him* when all *He* ever did was forgive and heal and preach love.

What if we find out, when we get there, that all this suffering is what washed out the meanness and worldliness that would have separated us from God? Find out it was the very suffering that formed our soul so that it *could* see God? What if our suffering is making us into saints who will weep for

234

joy forever that we were shaped by it? What if that is really the "secret" we have all been looking for?

But everybody wants to be happy. Hap hap happy all the time. Even when we entrust our lives to God, snaky little thoughts plague us, sizzling against our Godly resolve:

If God is so great, why did mother get cancer? If God loves me, why can't I lose weight? What about the terrorists and Aids and war and murder? The starving children in Africa?

Here's the big secret--He wants something a lot better than *happiness* for us and He wants it to last *forever*, not just the 70-more-or-less we'll put in here. *Joy* is His gift. Not what the world calls "happy." "Happy" is that little buzz our flesh gets when we feed its cravings. *Joy* is what our *soul* gets when we do something *holy* in His name. Big difference. Even if we are crushed beneath wheels of unspeakable suffering with the loss of a beloved, Jesus is the only one who gave us the promise we *will* see them again.

And God does not *send* the suffering. Gotta remember the "bad guys" have Free Will too. The devil still lurks about. And God certainly doesn't blame you for not *wanting* to suffer. Who would? What God *says* is that when you *do* suffer, you are united deeply with Him in an intimacy that cannot be attained any other way. And that He uses it somehow, to His own eternal, perfect end. In his letters to the first Christians, Paul put it clearly:

> *For I consider that the sufferings of this present time are not worthy to be compared with the glory that is to be revealed to us.* (Romans 8:17-19)

> *For to you it has been granted for Christ's sake, not only to believe in Him, but also to suffer for His sake.* (Philippians 1:28-30)

235

What was Jesus' mission? The cross.

What is *our* mission? The same as His. Jesus said it Himself:

"Whoever wants to be my disciple must deny themselves and take up their cross daily and follow me." (Luke 9:23)

We misfits likely got that way through our trials, our suffering. And, on its own, it is exactly what the world says it is: too bad, so sad, tsk tsk. But when we identify with Jesus, when we are *with* Him in His mission, then we are with Him on that cross. We are intimately identified with the God of the universe. It still hurts. It is still hard. But it has *meaning*. It is *holy*. We are cooperating with God in the salvation of the world.

WE ARE ON A MISSION FROM GOD

I know my own crosses very well. Many, many times through the years I asked God "why?" and told Him I couldn't take it anymore. Many times I thought maybe I was doing something wrong, since I was still suffering. What I know now is that suffering does not *come* from God. Bad things happen whether we are His or not. Crummy genes, bad neighbors, abusive relatives, and more. But if we stand still, if we have faith, if we surrender to Him, He turns it *all* to good. Always. (Romans 8:28)

Just today I suffered a bolt of rejection from a lifelong friend that only God Himself would understand. An agony of tears and bitter thoughts later, I came to Him with it. Shaped the invisible fiery ball of hurt and anger in my chest with my hands, literally, and held it up to Him. "Take it, Lord. I give it all to You. Thank You for Your love. Your love is sufficient for me. Turn this ball of rage and pain to Your good purpose."

And then walked away and put my mind to other things best I could. Limp, shaking, determined.

I swear to you, before all that is holy, He shaped my soul and mind to Himself in a new way. Letting it go was hard...my flesh is inclined to nurse these hurts a while. His grace is already answering the choice. He is bringing someone to me this very hour who needs what I did not ever get myself. I am healing already to give it to them. The only medicine I ever had for that. Ever.

There is a woman in our church who brings her adult daughter with her in a wheelchair to services. The young woman is brain-damaged, barely able to sit, incapable of speech. Her mother leans into her lovingly, touching her face, smoothing her hair, adjusting her pillows. Full of tender mercy toward her damaged child.

Don't you think God must have a special affection for *us* when *we* suffer? Sometimes His love will give us relief, even a cure. But *always* it will give us this same kind of tender love and care. I have felt it myself, when I suffer. Perhaps you have too. Everybody suffers something sometime. For nothing... or for the greatest story in the world.

> *Now I rejoice in my sufferings for your sake, and in my flesh I do*
> *my share on behalf of His body, which is the church, in filling*
> *up what is lacking in Christ's afflictions.* (Colossians 1:24)

Suffering can make a hardened criminal get on his knees. Or turn a self-absorbed narcissist into a tender friend. Or an arrogant businessman into a saintly philanthropist.

Success never does that. Or money. Or even robust good health. Only the cross the Lord designed just for us.

I always knew my heart was broken. The thing I had wrong was the belief that the Lord would *fix* it. That it wouldn't be broken any more. That if He really loved me, He would take away my suffering.

Nope.

He didn't fix Joni Eareckson Tada's paralysis either.

Or take away mother's cancer.

Or bring the Money Truck.

Or wave a wand over the addictions some Beloveds suffer from.

Or prevent death.

Any Hospice worker will tell you that terminal patients are almost always very spiritual. Nothing puts people in touch with spiritual life like death. No more delusions about this life.

We all lose Beloveds, or have terminal illnesses or face the specter of Death along with all our other forms of suffering in this fallen world. It keeps us humble, keeps us seeking, and keeps us looking up.

I kept my broken heart. It has its own tiny little wheelchair, my crippled heart. In a way, it defines me. Like Joni is "the crippled lady who paints with her teeth." We do what we still *can*.

Naturally, we would all rather be happy all the time. And it *feels* like God must not like us very much when we suffer. *But it simply isn't true.* It is a lie straight from the pit of hell, the whiny screeching of the damned trying to take us with them.

The Bible is full of beautiful passages about the glory of suffering *in Christ*. My favorite is this one:

> *...affliction is producing for us an eternal weight of glory far beyond all comparison.* (II Corinthians 4:17)

I can't tell you exactly what "eternal weight of glory" is, but it sounds awesome, and it sounds like forever. A glorious reward, for sure.

People looking in the window, who don't know, wonder why God wouldn't heal them. But that isn't the victory, you see. A person of *faith*, looking in the window, would say "look how they continue on in faith, in spite of their handicap. God's grace really *is* sufficient..." (II Corinthians 12:9).

Like Michelangelo chipping away relentlessly, lovingly on the huge slab of marble, our God shapes us. We may suffer in the shaping, but we are being made beautiful forever.

For now, we can choose to see the grace in the horror, the trust in the fear, the pony in the pile of manure.

We can quit asking "*why.*"

And actually *thank* Him for all we've learned the hard way.

Quit asking why there is suffering in the world, while we withhold our love, judge our neighbor, sit rigid in our warm pews, staring covetously at another's car or clothes.

Nope, nothing to do but trust Him with it all. Know in our spirits that someday we *will* know. Then our whole life here will seem, as philosopher and theologian Peter Kreeft puts it, "like one night in an inconvenient hotel."

The disciples suffered horrid deaths and stonings and prison...and the church grew from it. If Paul had not been in prison we wouldn't have most of the New Testament. If we ourselves had never been shaped or humbled by own sufferings, we would have been out playing video games and partying with friends instead of building our immortal souls.

In a land we have not seen or heard, He makes of all our sorrows, all the consequences of our sins, an "eternal weight of glory." A holy thing, He makes of it all, our Alchemist. Gold from the lead of our days here. Beauty from the ashes. His love overcomes everything.

And when we love, and forgive, and follow Him, suffer with Him, we become a part of Him. And overcome the world with Him.

So for now, we pick up our own crosses, and walk with Him to glory.

Because we will do for Love what we simply will not do for fear.

Dear friends, do not be surprised at the painful trial you are suffering, as though something strange were happening to you. But rejoice that you participate in the sufferings of Christ, so that you may be overjoyed when his glory is revealed. (1 Peter 4:12-13)

Chapter Fourteen

Making Holy

"Show, Don't Tell"...God's Best Theology

And even though it all went wrong
I'll stand before the Lord of Song
With nothing on my tongue but Hallelujah
--Leonard Cohen

So now we know the whole story. The one story big enough to give flesh to ideas too universal to comprehend.

We see how and why it happened. Separated forever from God's holy presence, the devil and his followers were cast down to fallen Earth like venomous spiders, and began to spin their web of bitter deceit.

Clever, dogged, and brilliant, their only delight from then on was to take others with them. Misery really does love company. Like any common spider, but on a cosmic scale, they laid traps out in the open, beautiful but deadly. Almost invisible.

Once a hapless soul is entrapped, the devil, like the spider on your porch, fills them full of venom that paralyzes them, makes them give up, quit struggling in the web. Like any addict you've ever known, helpless in the sticky, invisible deceit.

We begin to be able to imagine the whole world, all these thousands of years later, encrusted in layer upon layer of gossamer webs, the satanic star woven into an intricate pattern. Humans deluded, incapacitated, poisoned. Then, finally, consumed. Like the moth you watch being devoured in the web on your porch. Still alive, but helpless.

Now we get it. See it, maybe for the first time. Imagine Someone coming through the web. Clearing a path for their escape. Our escape! Cleaning us up and making us wiser about those dangerous webs. Helping us see how we are cherished, loved. Inviting us to call on Him if we become entangled again. Teaching us how to avoid the traps.

A new creature. Wiser now, beloved child of God. Seeing the evil web for what it is. Loving Him for coming to get us. Instead of angry at Him for the bad stuff that happened.

As a young girl, I fantasized about lying down in a clear creek bubbling over a pristine rock bottom, letting the water run over me. Cleansing me. Never felt I was who I was meant to be. Just not quite right. Sullied somehow. Encrusted in bad genes, bad habits, bad feelings and thoughts. But with an inner longing for how I wished I could be: Clean. Pure. Innocent. Not know the bad stuff I knew, not have seen the horrid things I'd seen, nor done the icky things I'd done. Erase all the crud, without erasing my Self.

It wasn't until I was deep into my new faith-walk that I understood this to be a desire to be *holy*. Instead of…whatever I knew myself to be. *Not* holy, for sure.

On the TV right now is a video of a toddler being run over by two cars in China, laying there bleeding in the road while people walk around her. History is full of people like Roman Emperor Caligula who killed his sister Drusilla after learning that she was pregnant with his child. And Hitler's gas chambers methodically killed 12 *million* human beings only a generation ago. In our own generation children are kidnapped and sold into sex trade slavery, brains of college kids eaten by cultists in Mexico, serial killers line the rivers and canyons with their prey.

Take nothing for granted; but for the grace of God there we all go. Like spoiled children who cry "look what you made me do!" when we fall, we want to blame God for the bad things that happen. But God is all good.

Evil destroys itself.

But we sure do hate the word "sin" in our culture today. The butt of jokes and sneering comments. The world tries to jolly us out of any notion of sin; nobody wants to be "judged." But there's just no getting around the effects of the ugly, damaging things that were done *to* us, or the guilt and shame from the things we've done. The things that wounded our souls, crippled our will. Made us misfits in this world.

Funerals for loved ones talk about Heaven. And many movies illustrate Hell.

Deep inside, we know it *does* matter how we live our lives.

Scripture says it clearly. But the world mostly talks and lives like it doesn't.

God, Jesus, and the disciples wouldn't have gone to such lengths to communicate the "dos" and "don'ts" if it didn't matter. But those of us here watching secular TV in this fallen world come to think it doesn't. We are left wondering what we are here for and why it matters.

Does God care how we live? Is there a goal, beyond faith? Beyond our salvation from Hell?

WHAT *IS* "HOLY"?

And why would we care?

The Bible tells the story, from the perfection of Eden, through the bloody sacrifices of the ancients, until the final bloody sacrifice of Jesus on that cross. It was always about the "blood." And about "sin." How it took one to cover the other.

And now we don't even know what the heck that means.

Is one sin "worse" than another? Hitler was, after all, way worse than the kid who stole your bicycle out of the yard. Most people understand *civil* laws and the consequences of breaking them. But not many think about *divine* laws anymore. Or the consequences of falling short of those.

And it *is* confusing sometimes. Not so black or white.

Think of it like two *magnets*...He is pulling us to Him all the time. The instant we turn to Him, *zap*, we're with Him. And the minute we turn away from Him, *zap*, we are repelled, *incapable* of coming near Him. It is all free will. True love always is. He never *compels* us against our will. But o baby, the instant we turn that will *toward* Him, He holds us tight.

"Monsters are real," Stephen King once said. "And ghosts are real too... they live inside us and sometimes they win." Yes, don't they though. But we know our journey now. And how much more beautiful "holy" is that the dark lies.

A PICTURE WORTH A THOUSAND WORDS:

Jesus Himself said "This cup is the New Covenant in My blood." (I Corinthians 11:25)

I never understood it until I studied the ancient rite, the "Blood Covenant." A blood oath simple as childhood pacts, complex as a legal document.

That's one thing we can always count on to get our attention: *blood*. Can't ignore it, can't look away. Salty, warm, sticky up close. Like animals, we can smell it. We don't always know what it "means" when we see blood. It tells its own story. Now we have hospitals and ambulances to hide it from us. But God's story is *written* in it.

Thousands of years before Christ, men could see for themselves that the life of a person or animal was in their blood. So when they wanted to join forces with another person, or another tribe, they "cut a covenant." And in their ancient rite we can see for ourselves what our sanitized, bloodless culture has forgotten. And *get*, maybe for the first time, what God actually *did* for us in His ultimate Blood Covenant. And maybe an inkling of what He expects us to do in return:

1. A representative of each tribe was chosen, the two faced each other, their people gathered behind them, and EXCHANGED ROBES. Their robes *identified* them, so with this act they exchanged *identities* with each other. They became *one*.

2. Each representative HELD UP HIS BELT. A belt in those days carried their weapons. This was their pledge to stand by the side of the other, defend them in battle. Anyone outside their tribes who fought one would fight both. All their assets were available to either party.

3. Then they CUT THE COVENANT. An unblemished animal—a ram or bull or the like—was split down the middle and laid between them, blood pooling at their feet. Each representative stepped *into* the blood, then turned their backs to each other and walked a few steps away, turned, walked back to each other. They then both pointed to the dead animal and vowed something like "May God (or you) do this to me if I ever break my covenant with you."

4. Then each one put up his right hand, then cut it with a knife, then they held each other's hands and EXCHANGED THEIR OWN BLOOD (the ancient precursor to our "handshake" deal). They are now "blood" relatives—family.

5. They EXCHANGED NAMES. Each added the other's name to his own, making a new name for each that included the other's.

6. They then rubbed their cut hands to MAKE A SCAR. From that point on, they could show the scar to anyone who bothered them and the other party honored it. They knew they had both tribes to deal with.

7. They ANNOUNCED THE COVENANT TERMS and all the blessings and curses for keeping or breaking the covenant terms before all the witnesses. Then said to each other: "All my assets are yours. If I die, all my children are yours by adoption. Everything I have is yours, at your command."

8. They SHARED A MEMORIAL MEAL. Bread and wine represented the animal's body and blood. They each broke the bread in half and fed the other, pledging that "We are one flesh now. I am in you, you are in me. We have a new nature now." (Wow, Christians. Wow. Now we begin to "get" communion, and what Jesus really did when He made the perfect Covenant on our behalf.)

9. They PLANTED A MEMORIAL TREE and sprinkled the wood with blood from the animal. (I don't imagine you need any help picturing the wood of the cross and His blood hundreds of years later.)

From that point on, they were *family*. They belonged to each other forever. A picture really is worth a thousand words.

We get whiffs of it when we see the metaphor in books and movies:

Harry Potter's mother, Lily, sacrifices herself to save Harry from Voldemort. And ultimately, Harry sacrifices himself for the good of all of Britain.

In "A Tale of Two Cities," the lawyer Sydney Carton gives his own life for prisoner Charles Darnay's. "It is a far, far better thing that I do, than I have ever done; it is a far, far better rest that I go to than I have ever known," he echoes the biblical substitution.

In the movie "Man on Fire" alcoholic bodyguard Creasy gives his own life to save the life of Pita, the kidnapped little girl.

In the WWII movie, "Saving Private Ryan," Captain John Miller gives his life to save the life of Private James Ryan, whose mother has already lost three sons to the war.

In "Gran Torino," Clint Eastwood's character, an aging war vet, comes to care for his Hmong neighbors and finally sacrifices his life in a hail of bullets to save them from a vicious local gang, his arms out like a crucifix.

In "The Mission," haunting music plays as a priest is sent down the huge waterfalls tied to a wooden cross...

BLOOD. DEATH. Sacrifice FOR OTHERS. We "get" it in movies. Know they are heroes.

And that can help us "get it" in the gospel.

Jesus *came* to be sacrificed. He suffered everything we suffer, was tempted by the devil like we are tempted. Fully God and fully man, He took His own blood and laid it on the altar in Heaven.

And by His sacrifice He became our *everything*. Our "tribe," family, source, provision.

Did it make us "holy"? Yes. Scripture is plain:

> "We have been made holy through the sacrifice of the body
> of Jesus Christ once for all." (Hebrews 10:10)

Now we have a sporting chance to live a life that does *not* "miss the mark" all the time.

Not perfect, none of us. Who is? But wrapped entirely in His perfection as a member of His family. And empowered by His Holy Spirit, to choose His way.

Those first misfits, cast from Eden, had to trudge out into the desert covered only by a few animal skins and God's promise that life was going to be hard. I know just how they must have felt. This life *is* hard.

It's been thousands of years since that bad day in Eden. It was verrrry expensive, that gift of Free Will. But He loved us broken humans enough, missed that evening walk with us in the Garden enough, to do all that for us.

God told us a *story* instead of a sermon, so we would understand. You cut a *dead* body, you will see no blood. You cut a *live* body...blood. Totally concrete, no sermon required. Adam and Eve knew what God *told* them in the Garden. Then, when they cut themselves off from God, they knew what their five senses told them—what they could see, hear, touch, taste, or smell. That blood said "life" to them. A picture worth a thousand words. Nobody had to explain to them what their rebellion cost.

EVEN IN THE MOVIES:

Missionary Don Richardson has written books about other cultures around the world and the cultural "redemptive analogies" that they have that helps them understand the gospel. In the book "Peace Child," he tells about two warring villages of the Sawi people and the only way they had of making peace: A father in one of each of the two villages made a stunning sacrifice. Each gave one of his own children as a "peace child" to his enemies' tribe. After that, no one wanted to harm the other's tribe, because they each held a precious child of the other.

Richardson was then able to explain the Christian gospel as the greatest father sacrificing the greatest son to make peace for the world. Those people *got* it. We can too.

It is why we love "The Prince and the Pauper" and "Cinderella" type stories and movies. Once a street urchin, now a wealthy prince. Once a servant, now a princess. Once a homeless ragamuffin, now a movie star. There are a million of them.

The eternal and best one being the GOSPEL. Because it is TRUE. *Concrete* facts about an *abstract* truth. Forever. And *we* don't have to *keep* it. Our mediator at the Blood Covenant is keeping it *for* us, on our behalf.

When I look back at my own life, the only parts I regret now are the ones lived apart from God's will. In younger years, mostly by ignorance, then, later, by willful disobedience or tepid faith.

Before Jesus died on that cross, God's "wrath" was all we could have expected. And eternity to regret it all.

But now?

"Therefore, there is now no condemnation for those who are in Christ Jesus." Romans 8:1

No condemnation?! For all the things we've done? Or failed to do?

None.

God's holy eternal presence always was incompatible with our sinfulness. Oil and water, for lack of a better analogy. *Not* that He is hiding in the bushes, mad, waiting to rain fire on us when we fall away, but that He cannot bring us in to His presence, His perfect love, when we do. We are adrift, subject to the vagaries of the world, the flesh, the devil—our sins and everyone else's. Sitting targets. He wants us to be a certain way for the same reason we teach our little children to stay out of the street.

Sin broke something in the universe. When Adam and Eve ate the fruit and knew Evil, they did not just know it in an abstract, purely intellectual way. They knew it physically, by experience. They worked, they suffered, they bled, and they died. Immortality became mortality. Removed from the vine of life in God, they became subject to the actual physical laws of the material world apart from the constant infusion of God's holiness. They knew it right away.

They would be poor, weak, vulnerable little animals indeed, scurrying about in the wilderness looking for food. Their lives would be so hard their children would scarcely believe their stories of Eden. And their grandchildren no doubt thought the old folks were senile. Soon, mankind was, in fact, *lost*. Separated from their Maker.

Until God came Himself, in human flesh, to make the Covenant that would change us back into creatures holy enough to be His family forever. A way to begin to put Humpty Dumpty together again. Repair the damage done in Eden. The way sinful man could still relate to holy God.

If a policeman doesn't see you break the *speed* limit law, you can get away with it. But if you jump out of a window hoping to break the law of *gravity*, you will be *broken*. The first is a "rule." You might get away with breaking it. The second is God's *reality*. Go against that and it breaks *you*. In ancient Hebrew that understanding was a given; it has been lost over the millennia, taken to mean mere "do's and don'ts." It is more than that. Because He loves us, He wants us to know. Just like we want our children to know not to walk into that busy street.

But what do we know about *blood* anymore? First sight of it, doctors, firemen, policemen and morticians whisk it away. But when the earliest men stood in the wilderness, they knew. They watched their animals, their children, and others die and they knew.

So began the Judeo-Christian history that would change the world. You have to understand these were ancient times. They did not have books or churches, they had not been to school. "Show, Don't Tell" was the only way to teach them. Show them the bloody consequence of sin—death. Show them, like in Exodus, how blood smeared on the doorposts kept the Angel of Death from taking the firstborn children. *Show them.*

And still is today. Those crosses on the wall, the baptismal fonts, the beads to hold, the candles to light. So many ways we can see and touch the things we do not entirely have words for. So many ways the Lord Himself gives us to remind us of His presence as we walk by.

If you had a child you had to visit in prison, or the cesspool back alley drug dens, in order to try again to convince them of your love, or the possibility for a better life, then you have a tiny inkling of why God pursued these unlikely people. Not because they deserved it, or were any better than anyone else in the world at that time. Abraham met Him in the desert, bringing only his faith. Moses met Him on behalf of the people out in the wilderness, dragging them whining and disobedient to the Promised Land. He still comes to meet us the same way. In whatever desert wilderness we have become ensnared in this fallen world.

Many days all we *can* do is show up with our faith.

All days that is enough.

Do we still sin? Of course we do. And even today, just like "haters gonna hate," it is also true that "doubters gonna doubt." Right up until they find themselves face-down in the dirt of their own mistakes and look up. And of course there really is a devil who loves only too well to keep bringing pictures of your sin up before your mind all the time. And lying to you all the time about how swell another round of it would be.

It's easy to see with addicts: one little whiff and lots of perfectly normal people are swept into a dark abyss of suffering day after day trying to renew a pleasure pathway in the brain that ain't *never* comin' back. Because the devil lies about how wonderful it will be. And we believe him instead of God.

Ditto with compulsive shoppers. And eaters. And pedophiles. And gambling addicts. And, of course, the one most people think of first: sex. I think people can even be addicted to negative thoughts and depression, because somewhere back there it got them the attention they craved.

TODAY'S WORST CUSSWORD

All those problems are not who we *are*. It is what we *do*. When we bumble along not knowing who we really are, we define ourselves by what we do. But in Jesus Christ we have a *new* identity. Jesus keeps the terms *for* us, we wear His name.

His forgiveness is a gift; we could never achieve it on our own. If you trust Jesus this far, He will certainly take you the rest of the way.

Jesus. It's a "cuss word" we hear all the time these days, isn't it? The world has tried to ruin His name, but I don't care, I'm taking it back:

Jesus.

You wanted someone to come for you.....Jesus did.

You wanted to be better than you are. Now you are brother or sister to the Creator God of the entire universe. You bear His name, His blood, His nature. A child of the King instead of a roadside beggar.

When you choose to live your *real* story, the one God is trying to tell, you walk into the only possibility for joy in this world. Then you will want to do things to share the wealth. Those are the "works" that will make it through the fire at the end.

God doesn't even remember our sins. He casts them as far as "east is from west," (Psalm 103:12) when we confess and come to Him.

And when we feel like a failure, sorry what we coulda, shoulda, woulda, we have it straight from Jesus Himself:

"The work of God is this: to believe in the one he has sent."
John 6:28-9

And that is our journey. A simple one for anyone whose mind is simple, a straightforward road, hard and true, for those who need it to be, and complex as String Theory for those who revel in the unfolding complexities of Truth. He speaks every "language" in the world. And He will speak yours if you ask Him.

He came and took His own medicine. Just like as if Daddy went to the jail and paid our fine for the speeding ticket we got.

Does Daddy wish we would *behave* better from now on?

Sure He does.

Does He love us anyway?

Of course.

Will He cover for us again if we ask Him to?

Yes.

Will we start behaving better, out of gratitude and love?

Yes. If we *choose* to.

It isn't the *world* the gospel changes.

No, it changes minds. Changes hearts and souls.

If we let it.

Can God use a sinful misfit?

Noah got drunk
Jacob was a liar
Joseph was abused
Moses had a bad temper
Gideon was afraid
Samson was a womanizer
Rahab was a prostitute
David had an affair and was a murderer
Elijah was suicidal
Jonah ran away from God
Peter denied Christ three times
The Disciples fell asleep while praying
Martha worried too much
The Samaritan woman was divorced, more than once
Paul was cranky and hard to get along with

Yes, I think so.

THE LAST WORD

All Shall Be Well

I cannot be disappointed.
I have no expectations apart from the Will of God.
~Ran Stovall

"What shall I say, Lord," I asked Him. "Your final Word to all us wounded misfits?"

"Hebrews 14," He smiled into my spirit.

I ruffled the pages to confirm my suspicion. Nope. Only thirteen chapters in Hebrews.

"My mistake, Lord?" I wondered.

No, His Spirit whispered into mine. *Everyone has to write their own last chapter.*

I smiled and nodded.

Yes. We do.

He never tells us we have to be like everyone else. Once we grow to love Him, trust His love, we begin to find our "true self" by dying to the *wounded* self we were stuck with before. Now that we know Him, believe His Word, trust His love, we are *free*. Free to *choose*. Write our own story. Our own last chapter.

Those hard first stories are still there: her mother's boyfriend shot her dead in front of her when she was only five...he found his father's bloodied body, gun still in his hand... a toddler herself, her baby brother died in her arms...her mother set her bedroom on fire while she slept...she was left with a strange man as a toddler and never had words for the disease and irrational fears...

Children tell their stories, too young to make them up.

Or hide them away in the basement of their souls until they are grown.

If they survive to tell them at all.

Big pile of steaming poo in the wilderness, we cry.

And yet, growing right out of the middle, my sweet brother reminds me--beautiful flowers.

How is that?

I meet people all the time who have gone under the waves for less.

Now that we know who we *really* are—God's beloved child—we are free to choose the rest.

More than "survivors," we follow Him and His words, limping, best we can, toward our forever Home with Him.

Broken, but blessed.

My goal in life now is to just lay back in His arms, be His little girl. Whatever time I have left is for that. Love the ones He gave me, steady the bridge for any who limp across to Him. Say "Your Love is sufficient for me" and mean it.

The Christian journey is like drawing a heart—the first strokes easy and joyful, then coming back down and around to the point. The main thing. The bottom line. Harder to make that second half come out just like the first, usually a little bent, a little less than we had in mind. Then back up into the point that says "heart."

Love. Not as perfect as we'd hoped, maybe, but a heart. *God loves me.* Like breathing, some days all we can do. *"God loves me."* If we believe only that, it is enough. Hard to do, when nobody else ever loved us...when we never even loved ourselves.

We learn to call Him "Abba," *Daddy*, and come to Him now without shame or secrets.

Churches still have problems, believers still get things wrong or walk in the flesh instead of the spirit. The world is still fallen, dangerous. Life is still hard. But we are heroes and heroines in the greatest story in the world now.

That's a lot.

It is, in fact, *everything.*

Like Jesus, that dark Friday, hanging bloody from that cross, we know for sure: *Sunday is coming!*

Now we can imagine our lost loved ones across that bridge to Heaven. A mystery lost in holy clouds. On my own, I see my friend Kitty, "God crazy" always, laughing that loving, manic laugh to see me again. And the good people who raised me well without quite being able to love me like "one of their own." Proud of me now with their new eyes, seeing how we are all filled with Jesus, not stuck in our disappointing flesh. My high school friend Nancy is there; she will have come the furthest, still generous to share everything she knows. And Mimi surrounded there, as here, by friends, and Gammie, still singing "Jesus loves me." Uncle Charley, grilling steaks with that gold-toothed grin. Stevie, gone too young, healthy and happy now. Beta so saintly, Grandpa my special friend. JoJo, fun and loving always, hugging her own with joy. And all seeing me for the first time like I *really* am. As I will them.

I will even see some friends from the Bible...Peter, my favorite "friend" because I recognize his impulsiveness and weakness--yet dogged faith like my own. And Teresa of Avila, who I know because of the burden of books and the burden of flesh, the mix of humor, all turned to good. Joan of Arc, mad and holy, knowing, like I know now, "if He is fire, I must be wood." Ignatius of Loyola who tells it like it is. And C. S. Lewis, whose books of faith and doubt held the bridge steady for me while I walked it years ago. So many more...like the Bible says, a great "cloud of witnesses."

Even my birth mother no longer a ruby-lipped stranger in a snake suit receding as an evil light on the horizon. Now when I notice the tiny light it grows larger and becomes the glowing light of a female figure and I am given to understand it is how she is now in heaven.

The evil done to her...
The evil she passed on to us...
Gone.
Transformed.
Like my own will be.
And *All Shall Be Well*
So now we face it. Quit pretending.
We surrender. Or not.
We trust Him. Or not.
Now we tell Him, as we walk to His light:

For all that has been, thank You.
For all that will be: Yes.

Ignatius, pray these words speak to people as yours have.
Teresa, thank you for the wisdom and humor in yours.
Peter, my friend, pray we all see how you had similar
wounded ways, yet were our Lord's chosen rock.

Acknowledgements

More like my love and undying gratitude forever! Not exactly for help with this book, but help getting me through life until I was able to write it:

My husband for being the Godly, hard-working, loving person I had to have to make it in this life. And to the Lord for sending him to me. Lord knows it's not that easy to love a misfit that well that long. So yeah. You will get stars in your crown for sure. XOXOXO

Our children, who bless us beyond imagining. Born to us by blood or given to us by our Lord, you all make our lives blessed. Worth it all. Giving what I never got really *did* heal so much in my ol' wounded heart. And you are all so solid in the Lord it is a joy *forever*. Not to mention *your* adorable, Godly children too! They make it *all* worthwhile, don't they? Forever hugs.

My twelve Beloveds whose names I cannot share. God knows and loves you. I love you too. It's been a hard journey, but we will know the *why* and the *riches* in Heaven. Together. Like Psalm 126 talks about...sow in tears, reap in joy. We did and we will.

And my relatives whom I love so much. Thank you for showing me what "normal" was over the years. Not "perfect," but the good and faithful and loving things none of us would ever have known without you:

Daddy, Mother, Walter, Betty, Gammie, Mimi, Hedy, Jane, Garry, Randy, Sherrill, Lisa, JoJo, Pam, Chelleye... Well, you know. So much fun. So much love and support.

My friends who gave me more than I could ever give them. More than they knew. Nancy, Kitty, Jan, Rosie, Dora, Mary, Pat, Linda, BJ, Jeanette. We are truly "sisters" in the Lord. Forever. Lots of fun, mayyyybe a little mischief, and a bond we will carry with us when we cross over to Forever.

And precious Maria Elena who was the loving, attentive precious soul I needed to help me raise my own family. Mother figure, grandma figure, safe right hand. God love you for it all. We all love you, "Nena"!

My brothers of every kind—adoptive, genetic, by marriage. Billy, Patrick, Larpy. Thank you more than you know. We understand each other better than most. You mean the world to me.

For all my friends on social media Groups out there who tell me "Yes! Thank you! Amen!" when another painful blog sheds the Lord's light for you too. It means a lot and you know who you are.

For Barrett for the joy of her victory in spite of her hardships, and the amazing way she continually gives to others. You are a miracle and a blessing. Hope you know this will all be part of *your* journey someday, too. As will your beautiful children.

And special thanks to those who did help with the actual book:

Mary Ann Gay for starting the "Social Media" and believing in the outreach. For always loving the Lord so sincerely, serving Him so earnestly. We all miss you so much, but know Heaven is richer for your presence.

To Barrett Hornbach for so much help with Social Media, blogs, and "on call" input. What would I have done without you? Lord knows, Lord rewards .

For Cari Caryl at Xulon Press for convincing me to publish it and solving many problems along the way. Muchisimas gracias!

And to Brandye Brixius, Salem Author Services, for rescuing me and seeing it through. Bless you!

Special appreciation for Grzegorz Japoł (grzegorz.japol@gmail.com) and his beautiful cover design and illustrations. The Lord knows who to get, doesn't He?

APPENDIX

Old and New Books That Blessed My Journey

Not a "Bibliography" exactly, because these days there are so many editions and publishers for the older classics and popular moderns. So just titles and authors! Find them anywhere, no matter what edition: Amazon, Barnes and Noble, eBay, and many online used book stores. They blessed me on my journey, maybe some of them would bless you on yours.

Alquist, Dale. G. K. Chesterton: Apostle of Common Sense.

Bunyan, John. The Pilgrim's Progress.

Chesterton, G. K. The Everlasting Man. [Or just look up "quotes" by him. Awesome.]

De Caussade, Jean-Pierre. Abandonment to Divine Providence. [An ancient treasure]

DeMuth, Mary. Not Marked: Finding Hope and Healing After Sexual Abuse. [If that was your trauma, you must read this one.]

Gallagher, Timothy, M. O.M.V. The Discernment of Spirits: An Ignatian Guide for Everyday Living. [The Ignatian description of "Desolation" and "Consolation" worth it all.]

Gillham, Bill. Lifetime Guarantee: Making Your Christian Life Work and What to Do When It Doesn't.

Hahn, Scott. A Father Who Keeps His Promises: God's Covenant Love in Scripture.

Hurnard, Hannah. Hind's Feet On High Places.

Julian of Norwich. All Will Be Well: 30 Days With a Great Spiritual Teacher.

Julian of Norwich. Showings. [Amazing story from amazing medieval mystic. Wow.]

Keller, Phillip. Lessons From a Sheepdog.

Kelly, Matthew. The Rhythm of Life.

Kreeft, Peter. Making Sense Out of Suffering.

Kreeft, Peter J., Ph.D. Jesus Shock. Beacon Publishing, 2012 [Oldie, goodie, harder to find but worth the search. Says it all, keeps it short.]

LaHaye, Tim. Spirit-Controlled Temperament. [Helps you understand *and* control yours.]

Leaf, Dr. Caroline. Switch On Your Brain: The Key to Peak Happiness, Thinking, and Health.

Lewis, C.S. Mere Christianity. [My personal favorite Christian book at beginning]

Lewis, C.S. The Great Divorce. [The best speculation about Heaven and Hell I ever read.]

Lucado, Max. When God Whispers Your Name.

Manning, Brennan. The Ragamuffin Gospel: Good News for the Bedraggled, Beat-Up, and Burnt Out. [Another misfit, saved by grace. Loved it.]

Meyer, Joyce. Battlefield of the Mind: Winning the Battle in Your Mind. [Says it all.]

Miller, Donald. Blue Like Jazz.

Paxson, Ruth. Rivers of Living Water.

Piper, John. Desiring God.

Piper, John. When the Darkness Will Not Lift: Doing What We Can While We Wait for God--and Joy.

Sayers, Dorothy. The Mind of the Maker. [If you like brilliant, read hers.]

Schrier, Priscilla. Fervent.

Solomon, Charles. The Rejection Syndrome and the Way to Acceptance. [Huge help]

Solomon, Charles. Handbook to Happiness.

Strobel, Lee. The Case for Christ: A Journalist's Personal Investigation of the Evidence for Jesus.

Van der Kolk, Bessel, M.D. The Body Keeps the Score: Brain, Mind, and Body in the Healing of Trauma. [Not Christian content, but the studies that prove it all and written with a good heart.]

Voskamp, Ann. One Thousand Gifts: A Dare to Live Fully Right Where You Are. [Lovely.]

Vujicic, Nick. Life Without Limits. [Boy, if *he* can do it, *we* can do it! Amazing.]

Walsh, Sheila. God Loves Broken People: And Those Who Pretend They're Not. [Soul sister.]

Warren, Rick. The Purpose Driven Life: What on Earth Am I Here For?

Young, Sarah. Jesus Calling: Enjoying Peace in His Presence. [My favorite *devotional*]

THE BIG WORDS

A Glossary of Sorts

I am not a theologian or a scholar. But there are many Bible words that I have read about and researched over the years. Here are some I thought worth sharing if you care to start your own investigation.

Every word has a story of its own, its meaning hammered out over hundreds, even thousands of years. Any one of them could be a life's work to study in its own right. Scholars over the centuries have studied these words to help explain the gospel to people.

Originally, in the ancient Hebrew pictographs, each word was meant to provide a "picture" in the mind of the hearer. A picture *is* always worth a thousand words. Jesus was good at that, teaching the deep truths in parables. Some of those word pictures have not survived the ages as well as others.

Our world is very different from the world two thousand years ago. But there are nuggets to be mined from them still. So here's the "big" Bible words that a Christian might want to understand. And some word "pictures" too:

ADOPTION

There are instances of adoption in the Old Testament, notably Moses and Esther, but there was not a Hebrew word for it until modern times. The Greek word *huiothesia* is translated "adoption" and is used several times in the New Testament. Louw and Nida's Greek Lexicon says: "to formally and legally declare that someone who is not one's own child is henceforth to be treated and cared for as one's own child, including complete rights of inheritance." So *huiothesia* literally means "to place as a son."

At the time the New Testament letters were being written, the prevailing law of the land was Roman. According to Roman law, a naturally born baby could be disowned from the family, but an adopted child could not. The parents knew what they were getting when they adopted, thus, permanently added them to the family. Many early Christians were Roman citizens, and using the word "adoption" conveyed the fact that God chose them and would never abandon them.

Further, since Roman children did not become full heirs until adulthood, the verses that use the word for "adoption" gave believers the assurance that they had all the full rights and responsibilities of adult sons, and were no longer treated as children or slaves, as before. This supports the idea of the previous Jewish "Law" being a sort of tutor, but Christ's adoption conveying all the full privileges of adult heirs.

When a child is adopted in the United States, his birth certificate and legal rights and name all appear just as if he had been born to the adoptive parents. The initial process can vary, but once that judge's gavel drops down, it is DONE. More a covenant than a contract. Becoming a member of the adoptive family conveys things a simple legal contract never could.

Likewise, once you are in Christ you are a child of God, with all the rights, privileges, and responsibilities. It is a FAMILY COVENANT. As His child, with free will, you will grow under the covenant of family love.

> *The Spirit you received does not make you slaves, so that you*
> *live in fear again; rather, the Spirit you received brought*

about your adoption to sonship. And by him we cry, "Abba, Father." Romans 8:15

So in Christ Jesus you are all children of God through faith, for all of you who were baptized into Christ have clothed yourselves with Christ. There is neither Jew nor Gentile, neither slave nor free, nor is there male and female, for you are all one in Christ Jesus. Galatians 3:26-28

So, when the Bible tells us we are "adopted," it is describing the act of God's grace by which he makes us a member of His redeemed family. Like any son or daughter, you inherit the protection AND chastisements, the trials AND the consolations of family life. He puts His Spirit in you, gives you a new nature. And, someday, you will inherit everything. All of these deep truths are found abundantly in scripture.

One thing that is interesting to an adoptive child is *where* he was adopted *from*. With us Christians, we were adopted *out* of Adam's family with the "sin nature" and *into* Christ's family with the *divine* nature. We were also slaves (to sin), and adoption makes us children instead of slaves. So we don't call Him "master" like a slave, but "daddy" (*Abba*) like a beloved parent. But as any adopted person can testify, we are *also* heir to the *sufferings* of our adoptive families. Ditto when we are "in Christ."

For all who are being led by the Spirit of God, these are sons of God. For you have not received a spirit of slavery leading to fear again, but you have received a spirit of adoption as sons by which we cry out, "Abba! Father!"

The Spirit Himself testifies with our spirit that we are children of God, and if children, heirs also, heirs of God and fellow heirs with Christ, if indeed we suffer with Him so that we may also be glorified with Him. Romans 8:14-17

Now I rejoice in my sufferings for your sake, and in my flesh I do my share on behalf of His body, which is the church, in filling up what is lacking in Christ's afflictions. Colossians 1:24

Adoption helps us see ourselves like God sees us, now that we are in Christ. That what God is after is our love relationship, not our fear. That we have a new IDENTITY in Him entirely. Yes, we will still suffer in this fallen world. But our Father waits with open arms to turn it all to good.

And we know that God causes everything to work together for the good of those who love God and are called according to his purpose for them. Romans 8:28

ADVOCATE

The Greek word *paracletos* is translated as "advocate" in the New Testament. It means "one called alongside to help; intercessor; one who speaks on behalf of someone." It is sometimes translated "Comforter," when it refers to the Holy Spirit, who now indwells believers.

Webster's defines an advocate as a person who speaks or writes in support or defense of a person or cause. An intercessor who pleads on behalf of someone, like a lawyer in a courtroom.

It is a name given by Christ three times to the Holy Spirit (John 14:16; 15:26; 16:7). It is applied to Christ in 1 John 2:1. And you can see Jesus

Himself actually in the act of *being* our "advocate" in John, chapter 17, where He is praying to God the Father on our behalf.

The Bible calls the devil our "accuser," so Jesus defends us before God.

In a nutshell, He is ON OUR SIDE, even if nobody else is.

ATONEMENT, ATONE

This word appears about 80 times in the Bible, most of them in the Old Testament. It means, in the religious sense, that obstacles to reconciliation with God are removed, usually through sacrifice. In Hebrew, 'to atone' (*kaphar*) means 'to cover', so the noun 'atonement' is a 'covering'. In Greek there are several different words used to convey the same idea, with the added nuance of "exchange" or "reconciliation" sometimes. To get real technical, Jesus IS the "atonement" for man's sinfulness. The Hebrew word for it was used a LOT in the Old Testament. It is used only a few times in the New Testament, always with reference to Christ's sacrifice. This atonement was the first step in reconciliation between God and man.

> *God presented Christ as a sacrifice of atonement, through the shedding of his blood—to be received by faith. He did this to demonstrate his righteousness, because in his forbearance he had left the sins committed beforehand unpunished.* Romans 3:24-26

> *For this reason he had to be made like them, fully human in every way, in order that he might become a merciful and faithful high priest in service to God, and that he might make atonement for the sins of the people.* Hebrews 2:16-18

So, instead of a bloody bull or goat in a "Blood Covenant" with God on our behalf (we are His "tribe"), JESUS was the blood offering, the perfect sacrifice. FOR ALL TIME.

The doctrines and traditions of various denominations differ in their language and understanding about atonement, largely because the New Testament used different connotations in different passages:

John 1:29 and Hebrews 9:6-14 have the idea of "appeasing" or erasing sin.

Matthew 8:17 conveys more the idea of substitutionary sacrifice.

Mark 10:45 more the idea of a "ransom."

Ephesians 1:7 of "redemption."

Romans 5:9 of propitiation.

So, don't be confused by the way different people talk about it. However it was used, the word meant that our "sin problem" was forever solved by Jesus Christ.

NOTE: "Expiation" and "propitiation" and "atonement" are ALL translated from the same Greek word *hilasterion*. Different theologians through the ages have, thus, emphasized different aspects depending on whether they believe sins are "covered" or "cleansed." In any case, they mean our sin problem was solved by Jesus Christ and we are reconciled to God through Him.

CHURCH

The Greek word translated as "church" in the New Testament is *ekklesia*. Depending on context, it can mean the local assembly of believers or the worldwide assembly of all believers. In either case, Jesus Christ is the *head* of the "church," and believers are the "body" of Christ. Scripture also makes clear that this "church" is the heir to all God's covenants with Israel:

...the Gentiles are fellow heirs and fellow members of the body, and fellow partakers of the promise in Christ Jesus through the gospel. Ephesians 3:5-7

And if you belong to Christ, then you are Abraham's descendants, heirs according to promise. Galatians 3:29

CONVERSION

Variations of the Greek word *strepho* mean to "turn." Essentially, it is an act of the human mind and will to turn away from his old flesh patterns and turn toward God's way. It is usually used to denote someone who was not a believer and becomes a believer, a "convert." It is not the same as salvation or regeneration, but it is necessary for them.

In the Bible there are instances where this conversion happens suddenly and instantly, as when Paul is converted in Acts, chapter 9. Other times, it is more gradual, with more help and preparation, as with Cornelius in Acts, chapter 10. In any case, it is when a person willingly tries to bring their heart, mind, and life into conformity with the will of God.

COVENANT

In Bible days, agreements between people were hardly ever written, as we do our modern "contracts." The terms of each party were spoken in a concrete ritual ceremony and could never be broken. Both parties asked God Himself to destroy them if they ever broke their terms. These covenants, spoken standing in the blood of sacrificed animals, made the parties blood kinsmen, with all the loyalty and love of a blood family. There were many *types* of covenants throughout the Old Testament, but only ONE "New Covenant" in the New Testament—Jesus' sacrifice on the cross on our behalf.

ELECTION

You will sometimes hear Christians referred to as "the Elect" or "God's Elect." The process that led to this state is called "election." The Hebrew word for "elect" in this sense comes from their word for "choose." In the Old Testament it is clear that ISRAEL was CHOSEN by God. Even though they were a small, ragtag, rebellious people, without merit of their own, His omnipotent Love just *chose* them to receive His revelation and salvation. They became His "elect." They constantly fell into unbelief and disobedience, but there was always a "remnant" of followers who were heirs to God's promises.

In the New Testament, followers of Christ are commonly referred to as "the elect." As such, they are also heir to all God's promises to Israel, because of Jesus' sacrifice.

The different denominations have different descriptions and/or explanations of just when this happens ("predestination" vs. "called" vs. "foreknown" etc.) and how much of our own free will is involved. But the bottom line is that God knew you and called you to be in His family.

EXPIATION

The means by which atonement is made.

The making of amends or reparations for something.

The reconciliation of man to God accomplished by Christ's permanent sacrifice.

This word was first used by theologians in the 15th century to DESCRIBE the atonement Jesus made on our behalf (see 'atonement' above). In the Bible itself, it is sometimes translated from the same Greek word (*hilasterion*) as atonement, so, technically they are interchangeable. In my mind, it comes clear when I think: "Jesus was the atonement, and that atonement was the expiation for our sin." The end result of which was our reconciliation with God.

Hilasterion is the Greek rendering of the Hebrew *kapporeth* which refers to the Mercy Seat of the Ark of the Covenant. *Hilasterion* can be translated as either "propitiation" or "expiation" which then imply different functions of the Mercy Seat. The English dictionary definition of "propitiation" literally means to "make favorable" and conveys the idea of dealing with God's wrath against sinners. Expiation literally means to "make pious" and implies either the removal or cleansing of sin.

GLORY

The word "glory" is used over 500 times in the Bible. *Kabod* is the Hebrew word for glory; it literally meant "weight." The glory of God is the "weight" of all that God is, conveying the ideas of very great praise, honor, fame, magnificence, radiance, exaltation. Sometimes represented as a halo or shining light surrounding someone. The glory of God is the beauty of His spirit. It is not an aesthetic beauty, but it is the beauty that emanates from His character, from all that He is.

Frequently in the New Testament it signifies a manifestation of the Divine Majesty, truth, goodness or some other attribute through His incarnate Son, as, for instance, in John 1:14: "(and we saw his glory, the glory as it were of the only begotten of the Father,) full of grace and truth"; Luke 2:32

When the Christian dies, he will be taken into God's presence, and in His presence will be naturally surrounded by God's glory. Our future glory when we are in Heaven was foreshadowed in the "Transfiguration," where, as told in the gospels, Jesus and three of his disciples go to a mountain. Jesus begins to shine with bright rays of light, then Moses and Elijah appear next to him and he speaks with them. It inspired awe in the three watching disciples. The living and the dead all alive eternally in God's glory.

To say that something is glorious indicates that it is just about as wonderful and perfect as it could be. That which has glory does not need to seek praise—anyone who sees it will naturally respond with praise.

GRACE

Grace is the unmerited favor and loving kindness of God. This grace is the bedrock of the Christian religion. "Sin" separates us from God, "redemption" is the process by which we are brought back, and "grace" is the means, and it is all God's.

During the years of the Old Testament, God's "chosen people" were trying to GET God's favor with their sacrifices and by keeping the "Law" that He revealed via Moses. The New Testament is a "Covenant of Grace." Essentially, it means that when we have our faith in Jesus Christ's sacrifice on the cross, we are standing in God's "grace," His constant, unmerited favor. And that when we think we are GETTING His favor by what we DO, then we are still under the OLD covenant of the Law.

Grace is God's very nature, His willingness to spare us the punishment we DO deserve and give us the salvation we DON'T deserve, through His son. He wants good for us. He is on our side. We do not have to tap dance to keep Him happy.

You cannot earn salvation with just your works, but there are "good works" that are the fruit of a true conversion to Christ. As opposed to "works of the Law."

> *"For by grace you have been saved through faith; and that not of yourselves, it is the gift of God; not as a result of works, so that no one may boast. For we are His workmanship, created in Christ Jesus for good works, which God prepared beforehand so that we would walk in them."* Ephesians 2:8-10

The first Christians were Jews who had labored under the infinite requirements of the "Law" for generations, and some pagans who were weary of appeasing multiple mythical "gods." So the new covenant of God's GRACE was awesome news, and many happily went to their deaths to defend it, preferring death in God's grace to endless tap-dancing to keep statue deities and emperors appeased. Many Christians today have wandered back into "keeping the Law" in some areas, as well, forgetting the freedom we have in Christ:

> *It was for freedom that Christ set us free; therefore keep standing firm and do not be subject again to a yoke of slavery.* Galatians 5:1

JUSTIFICATION (see also RIGHTEOUS)

The word for "justification" is only found in the New Testament, all in the book of Romans. It is from the same Greek root word as "righteousness" and denotes an attribute of God—His faithfulness, truthfulness, "justness." And, consequently, that believers are declared "justified" before God through Christ. "Justification" has become the darling of theologians. For 1500 years, the Catholic church had taught that when God "justifies" us by faith, we are *changed* into a divine child, God' grace is *infused* into us. The Reformation introduced the thought that we are not so much changed as COVERED OVER by Christ's righteousness...called "imputed righteousness." Either way, we are declared "justified" or "righteous" before God through our faith in the work of Christ on the cross. "Righteousness" is a person named Jesus. And "justification" is the word that describes how we are made righteous before God's perfect justice and righteousness.

The other sticking point between doctrinal understandings of justification is whether any "works" are necessary on our part or if it is entirely Christ's work on the cross that makes us "justified" before God. All agree, and scripture is abundantly clear, that justification is primarily and freely by faith. Some go on to say that this justification will be *evidenced* by "good works," as it say in James "Faith without works is dead." But also says many places, as in Ephesians, "By grace we are saved through faith." The Catholic understanding has been to leave these all as part of the "justification." The Protestant understanding has separated the "good works" into a separate process understood as "sanctification." But it is a natural understanding, in any case, that an obedient child will freely do the chores assigned by a loving parent.

> *For by grace you have been saved through faith; and that not of yourselves, it is the gift of God; not as a result of works, so that no one may boast. For we are His workmanship, created in Christ Jesus for good works, which God prepared beforehand so that we would walk in them.* Ephesians 2:8-10

These "good works" that God calls us to are not the same as the "works of the Law" that the Jews had to keep before Christ. They had been in bondage to the Law, and now they were free in Christ. The first Christians, mostly converted Jews, were overjoyed at that new freedom, happy to be released from the infinite points of Law described and enforced by the Pharisees. Still, today, some would rather chastise a child in church for chewing gum than tell him how much Jesus loves him. But it is still true that we will do for love and grace (of Christ) what we will never do for fear (of God's wrath).

The main thing you need to see about justification is that it means God sees you as clothed with the very righteousness, merit, perfection of Christ. We are, literally, clothed in Him before God. When we go to Heaven, and Father God says "stand up Jesus," we will all stand up. Because we are in Him, we are His body.

KINGDOM

The Kingdom of God (Greek: *Basileia tou Theou*) or Kingdom of Heaven (Hebrew: *Malkuth haShamayim*)

Jesus said that the Kingdom of God is within you (Luke 17:20) and is entered by receiving it like a child (Mk 10:15), spiritual rebirth (John 3:5), and doing the will of God (Mt 7:21). It is a kingdom that will be inherited by the righteous (1Cor 6:9). And JESUS is the KING of this kingdom:

> *"Jesus answered, My kingdom is not of this world. If My kingdom were of this world, then My servants would be fighting so that I would not be handed over to the Jews; but as it is, My kingdom is not of this realm." Therefore Pilate said to Him, "So You are a king?" Jesus answered, "You say correctly that I am a king. For this I have been born, and for this I have*

come into the world, to testify to the truth. Everyone who is of
the truth hears My voice." John 18:36-7

The ancient Jews were expecting an *earthly* kingdom, with Messiah as a triumphant King who would defeat the Romans. The Kingdom that Jesus ushered in was not like that; He was a 'suffering servant' instead of a conquering army. Many a saint has died with His words on his lips: "My kingdom is not of this world."

PROPITIATION

For hundreds of years before Christ, the Jewish people had the "Ark of the Covenant," where God met with the High Priest once a year on the "Day of Atonement." The "Mercy Seat" was a pure gold covering on TOP of the Ark. This is where the High Priest sprinkled the blood of the sacrificed animal in order to remove the sins of the people so that God could commune with them there. It has been called the "place of propitiation." Christ is now a *permanent* "Mercy Seat" for us. As our eternal "High Priest," he has removed the barrier of sin so that God and man can commune once again. No further sacrifice is necessary. He is the permanent, perfect sacrifice.

Many studies of this important Bible concept employ the notion of "appeasement." Like God is just *mad* and we are obsequious waiters trying to get Him in a good mood again. It is so much *more* than that. With Jesus' blood, God *removed* the barrier that sin created between God and man when Adam chose his own way.

There is no longer any impediment to man's return to God. The rest is up to the individual person. But God, for His part, is never-changing. He wasn't in a bad mood and is now in a good one. The sin of Adam and, consequently, the whole race, actually made man *unable* to live in God's presence, His "environment," so to speak.

God never changed; He was always love, He was always full of compassion toward his creatures. But He had to do something to make *man* change so that people could enjoy His presence again. This is how God forgives sinners without losing his own perfect righteousness.

"Expiation" and "propitiation" and "atonement" are ALL translated from the same Greek word *hilasterion*. Different theologians through the ages have, thus, emphasized different aspects depending on whether they believe sins are "covered" or "cleansed." In any case, they mean our sin problem was *removed* by Jesus Christ.

PROTOEVANGELIUM

"I will make you enemies of each other; you and the woman, your offspring and her offspring. It will crush your head and you will strike its heel." Gen 3:15.

God spoke these words to Satan as He exiled his first human family from the Garden. The battle between Good and Evil had begun. These words, so long ago, are called the "Protoevangelium," or the first *good news* of the Messiah Redeemer to come. With these words to the serpent (the devil), God revealed His plan to save the human race in spite of their sin. God's first response to man's sin, contained in Genesis 3, shows He is both infinitely just and infinitely merciful; He hates and punishes sin, but also loves man and will stoop to save him. His good will ultimately triumphed over this evil.

In the old covenant this ancient announcement was kept alive in the sacrifices, ceremonies, prophecies, and history of Israel, God's "chosen people." God never abandoned the human race to the power of sin and death they unleashed with their rebellion. He always wanted to save them. Then, with the crucifixion of Christ, it was accomplished. As the apostle Paul put it: "As by one man's disobedience many were made sinners, so by one man's obedience many will be made righteous" (Rom 5:18).

Early church fathers saw in the "woman" of the "protoevangelium" the mother of Christ, Mary. She was the new Eve (just as Christ is the new Adam). Jesus did what Adam failed to do. And Mary, through her "yes" to God, did what Eve had failed to do as well.

RANSOM (see also REDEEM)

In common usage, a ransom is the price paid to rescue someone from captivity or bondage. In the Old Testament, the Hebrew word for "ransom" and also for "redeem" means much the same thing—the idea being to set captives free.

To go deeper into the Bible truths of Jesus' ransom (and our redemption), do a word search on the internet for "kinsman redeemer." This was an ancient Hebrew way of setting slaves free:

Ways a person BECAME a slave:

He might he born into slavery.

He might be captured by a foreign army and sold as a slave.

He might get so deep in debt that he had to sell HIMSELF into slavery to pay the debts that he owed. He can only regain his freedom when the price of redemption is paid.

He could also be redeemed by a blood relative—a "kinsman redeemer"—who had the following qualifications:

1.   He must be a kinsman.

2. He must be free himself.

3. He must be able to pay the price.

4. He must be willing to pay the price.

Jesus fulfilled these requirements by taking on flesh and becoming a man. He was free from the bondage of sin. He was able to pay the ransom price. He was willing to pay the price. He is our "Kinsman Redeemer."

REDEEM REDEEMED REDEMPTION REDEEMER
(see also RANSOM)

Variations on the word "redeem" (from Hebrew for "to deliver" or "sever" from Greek for "loose; release" esp. by paying a price) appear about 150 times in the Bible, and have always been in common usage among Christians. The Old Testament prophesied a coming "Redeemer" and the New Testament proclaimed that redeemer was Jesus Christ of Nazareth. Most people are clear on that. What is fuzzy in our cultural thinking is just what that *means*.

Webster's dictionary says redeem means "to buy, pay back, and recover" and lists synonyms as "repurchase, redeem, ransom." The Bible tells us we are slaves to sin because of our "sin nature" we inherited from Adam. Also, that we are in bondage to Satan, the "god of this world." NONE of these conditions can be "fixed" by ourselves. God did it *for* us through His sinless son, Jesus.

God created man "in His own image" (Genesis 1:27) and walked with him in the Garden of Eden. But instead of living in God's friendship, he sinned—"fell"— and so became a *slave* of sin (John 8:34) Any addict can tell you that when you turn away once from the right choice, the wrong choice gets a stronger grip on you; finally, you *are* enslaved by those wrong choices.

When the New Testament uses "redemption," then, it is saying that Christ's death paid the price which set man free. So it is helpful to understand the "ransom" idea (above), i.e., the way slaves were "set free" or "redeemed." God's word was using imagery that had immediate clear meaning to try to HELP people understand His story. But today, we have few analogies like that. Maybe a Pawn Shop comes close. You take something valuable in and they lend you some money and *keep* it until you *PAY BACK* the charges plus the money they lent you. If you don't come and pay those charges within a certain time, you forfeit the item you took in.

Adam and Eve forfeited their gifts of innocence, immortality, and infused knowledge when they chose to believe the serpent instead of God. Without those qualities, they also lost the ability to live in direct communion with God, who is the pure source of those qualities. (Let's be clear: GOD did NOT walk away from THEM. THEY walked away from GOD.) Humans were never able to "redeem" themselves, get back those qualities they had "pawned" to the devil. Until Jesus. Jesus was able to buy them back. Not a perfect analogy, but food for thought.

REPENT

The Greek word for "repent" (*metanoeo*) is made of the root word for "change" and the root word for "the mind." The Bible says God is willing to forgive us when we repent, or turn from our sins in sincerity. It is necessary to faith, and, thus, to a true "conversion" to God.

When men see two ways they are then free to choose one over the other; they "repent" of the one and put "faith" in the other. That is, simply, what we do when we see our sinful, fleshy ways as a dead-end, and God's way as eternal Truth. Now, you can SEE it and NOT choose to walk in it. Maybe that is what the Bible means when it says "belief" is not enough. (James

2:19 "You believe that God is one. You do well; the demons also believe, and shudder.") Throughout the Bible, God's people fall away from His way and choose their own (remember the golden calf when Moses came off the mountain with the Ten Commandments). But all He seems to require is that they REPENT and turn back to Him. He is not a mean master, but a loving father.

RIGHTEOUS (see also JUSTIFICATION)

The Hebrew word for righteousness, *tzedek*, meant integrity, equity, justice, straightness. A person is "righteous" when he is upright, just, straight, innocent, true, and sincere. The Greek noun *"dikaiosune"* in the New Testament is used to denote God's unchanging attributes of truthfulness, faithfulness, holiness, justice, innocence, etc.—and is used in various cognates to describe anything that conforms to His perfect will. There are only two ways for a person to achieve this kind of righteousness—either through perfect adherence to the Law of the Torah, as in the Old Testament OR through faith in Jesus Christ's fulfillment of all God's law and righteousness, as in the New Testament.

Adam and Eve must have had this kind of righteousness, shared it with God there in the Garden. And LOST it when they obeyed the devil instead of God. God, loving father that He is, has been trying to give it back to us ever since. But only Jesus was ever able to maintain all those attributes in sinless perfection, be in perfect harmony with God the Father ("the Father and I are one"). Now, Christians can be "one" with Christ and thus "righteous" enough to be in God's family again.

Again—God never turned his back on us, his creatures. We turned away from Him and turned into something that was incompatible with His very essence and His presence. He has been trying to get us back—"reconcile" us to Him—ever since. He had to make us RIGHTEOUS first. And when we could never do it on our own, He became righteousness ON OUR BEHALF. He "enfleshed" Himself so He could pay human debts as a human, but do it perfectly, as only God could.

SACRIFICE

We have only a vague notion of how naked natives sacrificed virgins, and how the Greeks and Romans sacrificed various things to various deities for favors. But today we have no concept of a sacrifice of that kind at all. So how can we possibly understand the supreme, eternal sacrifice that God made of Himself in Jesus? We have no cultural analogies. Oh, we might drop a few dollars in the collection plate at church, and we know we have to "sacrifice" things to raise our children well. But that's about it. It is a huge gap in our ability, misfits or no, to understand the gospel. Jesus died on a cross; but so did a lot of other people, executed by the Romans. He made the sacrifice that somehow saves us. How was *His* different from *theirs*?

Bottom line: Because He was divine and because He took *His* all the way to Heaven.

You see, sacrifices, from prehistoric times, were all about the blood. (See Chapter Five, "Making Holy") When the earliest men stood outside in the splendors of nature, gazing at the infinite glory and mystery of the stars in the sky, they knew, just like we do, that it did not just appear. They knew there had to be something FIRST, that someone CAUSED all that. And they called that someone different names. And they wanted to communicate with that creator. They understood that they did not hold the power of life and death. They watched their animals, their children, die and they knew they were powerless over that breath that left their bodies, that blood that poured from their veins. We would do the same. We do. Whatever we believe, it is our instinct to look to "someone" to beg for mercy, ask for favors, blessings, thank for relief. It is removed more nowadays, because we have doctors and lawyers and psychiatrists to go to first, Welfare to provide a safety net. But when there was no one between the man and the vast unfathomable mystery, they turned first to Him.

Different pagan cultures developed different gifts to their deities as a sign of their veneration and desire for communion with him. And when they completely changed it—killed it and emptied the blood, burned it, or poured it out like wine or oil—then it was a "sacrifice." It was something that was of value to THEM that they offered to the invisible GOD they wanted to appease.

Have YOU ever thought maybe God was mad at you? Or wished He would do something for you? Of course you have. We human snowflakes are no two alike, yet all with the same molecular structure, the same yearnings and doubts. From cavemen to stockbrokers, men have longed for help from above, whether they felt gratitude for blessings or not. Always they have wanted to know. Always they have made their sacrifices, trying to get up to Him somehow.

But only once, in all these thousands of years of human history, did a god ever come down from heaven to try to meet US. None of the pagan idols, statues or invisible gods ever came to them. Not Buddha or Krishna or Ra or Zeus' not Vishnu or Shiva or Zoroaster or Moloch or Bear or Horse or anything the pagans ever fashioned into gods ever came down from heaven to reveal himself to man.

About 4000 years ago, in an ancient land called "Ur," where the Mesopotamian god Anu was worshipped, human sacrifice made to the moon god Nanna, God called a shepherd named Abram out of pagan Ur, promising to bless him and his clan.

And by faith, Abram went. God tested his faith by asking him to sacrifice his only beloved son, Isaac. And when he took steps of obedience, God stopped him, provided a ram for the sacrifice, and thus started the Judeo-Christian Biblical history that forbade human sacrifice until the one supreme one would come. The Druids and devotees of Moloch and other pagan religions around the world continued human sacrifice. But as God revealed Himself to the ancient Jews, it was never again allowed.

The Old Testament tells the long and often bloody history of God's "chosen people." Many of the stories offend our modern sensibilities. But the people God had chosen to reveal Himself to were a ratty lot to begin with— bloodthirsty tyrants, ignorant shepherds, and worse. There was no uniform moral law or code and pagan practices had to be overcome. Even so, it is hard going, hundreds of years of exile and return, victory and failure, God herding them like cats through the wilderness to mold them into people He could once again have a relationship with. A far cry from the daily walk in the Garden He created for them, and hard going. But His mercy, His love, His desire to have them for his own once again was behind it all. He allowed them to relate to Him in ways they understood—sacrifice and incense and altars—to prepare them for the day that HE would provide the ultimate sacrifice that would bridge Heaven and Earth forever.

The one where God sacrificed HIS only son on behalf of all men who put their faith in him.

God, the creator of the universe, long after he exiled his ancestors from the first Garden, returned to lead them back into His presence once again. He revealed himself to the nomadic shepherd named Abram, made a Covenant with him, and led him out of pagan bondage and into a life of faith and obedience. He began to shape and mold His chosen people through another two thousand years of exiles and returns, Covenants broken and renewed, Patriarchs, Prophets and Kings.

We call them the Jews. The Hebrew people. That same Abram God gave a new name, Abraham, and promised his descendants would number more than the stars. And Isaac had a son named Jacob, who God renamed Israel. And Israel had 12 sons, the "twelve tribes of Israel" history calls them. One of them, Joseph, again sent into Exile, who would later save his people and lead them out of bondage once again. Another one of them named Judah, through whom Jesus lineage can be traced.

So began the faith covenants between God and people, in the desert not far from modern day Baghdad, Iraq. None of the pagan gods had ever come to man. None ever provided the sacrifice himself, to meet the standards of justice he himself wove the universe from in the first place. None of them was ever alive in the flesh, then dead in the flesh, then alive again before them. THIS God is the one who created the universe, a perfect Garden, whether metaphor or roses.

In Old Testament days, from the first revelation to Abram, until the fall of the Jewish Temple a few years after Christ, the Jewish people had only one way to reconcile sinful man to God—blood sacrifice. The "peace offering" or "communion sacrifice" is described in Leviticus. A repentant person, sincerely wanting to be forgiven his sin and reconciled to God, brought an animal to the altar—often a lamb. He put his hands on the animal victim, identified himself with the animal, then slaughtered it, thus surrendering his own life vicariously through the animal's. He drained the life's blood into containers which the Priest then sprinkled on the altar. Then he placed some of the meat on an altar fire and burned it, the smoke symbolizing the life surrendered to God. Some of it was removed before it was destroyed, and eaten, symbolizing communion with God. The fire consumed God's part, the penitent and/or Priest on his behalf consumed the portion.

Jesus Christ fulfilled all these elements when he went to the cross. He was the "High Priest" who offered the sacrifice, and He was the sacrifice itself. He became the perfect sacrifice for all time. No other sacrifice will ever be needed for man to be reconciled with God. All impediments of sin and death which entered the Garden so long before were removed.

SALVATION SAVIOR SAVED

The word salvation appears nearly 200 times in the Bible. It was the entire purpose of every odd things told in the Old Testament, and entirely fulfilled in the New Testament by Christ. It includes everything done by God in all three aspects—Father, Son, Holy Spirit—to redeem people from the curse of sin and death, bring them back into communion with Him. It includes what the Bible describes as justification, sanctification, and eternal life in glory with Him. It includes atonement, reconciliation, repentance, redemption, expiation, propitiation...all the special words we have to describe the way God loved His frail little creatures, mankind, and brought them back into relationship with Him, brought them, over thousands of years since Eden, back to their only true Father.

In the Hebrew of the Old Testament, the words for salvation are used in various contexts to mean freedom from restriction, help from God, victory in battle, overcoming evil—rescue from anything that plagues a person or does not honor God.

The New Testament word for salvation in the Greek language is *sozo* or *soteria*, whose meaning is "healing, cure, recovery, remedy." God "saves" man by sending His son, Jesus, to die as the perfect sacrifice for sin. We are thus "saved" and "justified" and "reconciled to Him." Made RIGHT with GOD. Made RIGHTEOUS like Him. This "salvation" by our "savior" is outside time, past, present, and future:

We WERE saved from all penalties of sin.

We ARE BEING SAVED from the power of sin in our lives (also called "sanctification").

We WILL BE SAVED from the very presence of any sin when we are with Him in Heaven.

Our "salvation" begins with God. Through no merit of our own, God's grace, through Christ, has opened the way back to Himself. Each person can accept or reject this grace, choose to repent and follow God or choose to remain in his separated state. God will never take back His gift of free will. His love IMPELS, but it never COMPELS.

When a person responds to God's truth and turns to Him, trusts Him to make him His own through Christ, he is "justified." Reconciled to God. He becomes a child of God, an "heir" to eternal life. The doctrines of various denominations vary in their details, but whether it happens by reason or sacrament, it is the person's FAITH in God's act through Christ that changes their IDENTITY. No longer a child of this fallen world, slave to sin, but a child of the King, heir to all the riches of glory.

The rest of the person's life, they continue to choose how to walk—by faith, in the Spirit of God, or in the flesh, like they did before. This is one major way different denominations doctrines clash, as they try to describe this struggle of the Christian's walk. Catholics includes "works" as part of the person's "justification." Protestants have separated this process from the initial "justification" and call the continued walk and good works "sanctification." However you parse it, however, God has provided everything we need for us to be in His family. Forever. We choose it by faith, follow it in obedience.

Salvation, then, includes justification, sanctification, and eventual glorification. It is everything God accomplished, ultimately, through Christ and the indwelling Holy Spirit, to undo what Adam and Eve did, and make us part of His family again--forever.

SANCTIFICATION

In both the old and new testaments, the Hebrew word *qadesh* and the Greek work *hagiasmos* and their various forms mean the process of making or becoming holy, set apart for God. From the Latin verb *sanctificare* which in turn is from *sanctus*--"holy" and *facere*--"to make." It is the progressive transformation of the believer into the Lord's likeness or nature.

The million little choices of a believer take him closer to God's will for his life, or further away. As he chooses to walk in God's Spirit, the process is called his "sanctification." But he still has his "flesh," and often fails. God has promised, through Christ, to forgive us those sins when we confess them. So this daily faith walk seeking God is making us holy or "set apart" for a holy purpose. Theologians sometimes describe it as part of our justification with God, sometimes as a separate process. But in any case, it is part of our "salvation" in general.

SIN

This is a particularly "Christian" word, because, apart from scripture, we don't know how offensive to God our actions can be. Doctors and counselors call it "weakness" or "ignorance" or "illness" when we think or behave in aberrant ways. But when we put our thoughts and actions up against the yardstick of God's PERECT will, His clear instructions, we see how far we miss the mark.

Several different Hebrew words are used to describe "sin" in the Old Testament, and generally mean close to the same thing as the NEW

Testament Greek work for "sin" —*"hamartia"*—which is "to miss the mark." The inferior party breaks a covenant. Failure, rebellion, inability to keep a moral code. To a Christian, it means the failure to achieve God's perfection. Our only chance of doing that perfectly is in Christ, who was able to. When we fail, God has promised to forgive us and cleanse us because Jesus has already atoned for it.

Romans 14:23 is plain: *"....whatever is not done in faith is sin."*

I John 1:9 *"If we confess our sins, he is faithful and just and will forgive us our sins and purify us from all unrighteousness."*

A lie is a spoken perversion of reality. A sin is a lived perversion of God's Truth (reality) by actions. It is an offense to God in the same way a rape is an offense to woman. A perversion of what was created to be moral and good, to the shame, detriment and guilt of the perpetrator.

If there were a visible line between "Good" and "Evil" we could tell when we step over it, miss God's best will. Some, through pride or vanity, rebellion, self-centeredness, CHOOSE to live on the "Not God" side. But even believers are not always sure or strong in their will. Today, we have had the influence of God's truth through Christ active in the world for over two thousand years now. We cannot remember the vile and hopeless moral state of the pagan world before that. Now we take His standards almost for granted. But for the grace of God, there go ALL of us.

Before our salvation, "sin" was our very *NATURE*, the one we inherited from Adam and Eve. Like a criminal becomes a prisoner, men who seek their own way, apart from God, become "sinners." After we put our faith in Christ's work on the cross, that nature is changed. We have a NEW nature, a new identity. Now, when we "sin" it is an action that we confess and God forgives. Now we have the Holy Spirit guiding us to make choices TOWARD God instead of away from Him.

CPSIA information can be obtained
at www.ICGtesting.com
Printed in the USA
FFHW012325041218
49751552-54210FF

9 781545 644096